STEPS TO

After reading this book, you will kno
clearly walks you through how to build trust and confidence
with the Meeting Planner so they want to do business with
you.

Andy Dolce
Owner and Operator of Dolce Hotels & Resorts
Voted one of the "Top 25 Most Influential Executives"
in the Meetings Market.

I was chasing a corporate client for 3 years, each year filling
out the RFP and bidding on their business but not winning it. I
worked with Ciara, I implemented just three of the strategies
she recommended and boom. I won 75% of that client's
meetings business for this year.

Heather Thornton
Director of Sales, Yew Lodge Business Solutions, UK.

I have completed my review of your training materials. I
think they are absolutely fabulous as is. I don't think there is
anything I would change.

Jessie States
Manager of Professional Development
Meeting Professionals International.

Ciara has a brilliant way of focusing you on the client and
making the sale all about them.

Sally Lopez
Regional Director of Global Sales
Hard Rock Hotels, Europe.

We are always trying to get an edge, trying to figure out how to make Meeting Planners happy and win their repeat business. I really want to know their hot buttons. This is great because we get to learn what drives them nuts. We came up with a game plan, some bullet points. Some great things to apply with the team in Texas.

David Townsend
Director of Conference & Convention Planning, San Louise Resort,
Galveston Convention Center, Texas, USA.

Opened Up a Whole New Market!
Ciara helped us to open a whole new market segment that we hadn't considered possible for our hotel. We converted two conferences within a few weeks of applying her advice and tips. She just made it easy.

Tara Cronin
Vienna Woods Hotel, Cork, Ireland.

I certainly can relate to everything you are saying and believe you really understand the business when you highlight points about it all being about "YOU" and being passionate.
Passion to me, is definitely the secret of everything we do.

Ciara Mundrow
Head of International Affairs, European Society of Cardiology.

To my lovely man Michael. For your unwavering support and belief in me, even on the days when I lost it in myself. For giving me the time and space to get this done and mind our lovely boys Aaron and Jack. Thank you Jack and Aaron for being so good for Mammy and letting me write like a crazy woman when I had an idea.

Conversion Rates in Our Industry

I will always remember the wise words of John Simonich, a Regional Vice President of Operations at InterContinental Hotels: "Ciara, selling a hotel is a lot like selling perishable goods. If you don't sell a guest or meeting room today, the opportunity is lost forever." I've always looked at hotel sales from that perspective - the opportunity lost. It's helped me focus on the conversion rate, a key area I help my clients grow.

In our industry, the average conversion rate is 20%; that means 80% of sales effort is unproductive.

That adds up to a lot of empty guest and meeting rooms. Wasted sales efforts and empty rooms cost the industry billions in revenue opportunities every year. I wrote this book out of pure frustration in seeing why and how business was being lost. I was a hotelier, and I have walked in your shoes. I only saw the reasons why so much business is lost, once I became the client however. I share that perspective in this book.

I've calculated the **cost of leaving a conference room empty**. It runs into millions if you consider a conference room with a value of $20,000 a day being empty just two days a week for a year - **$40,000 a week, $160,000 a month.**

What is that worth to your profit line?

Why This Matters

I found writing this book the most therapeutic exercise I have ever done. It gave me clarity. It enabled me to get everything out of my head. It freed up my mind for even better ideas.

While I was writing this book, I realized that I had a system - the **Conference Converter System™** - made up of the **7 Steps to WIN**. This book details three of those steps, and all seven are the basis of my online academy, where I teach hotels and venues the "**7 Steps to WIN More Market Share from Your Competitors**." I work with sales professionals around the world and delight in the results they achieve from being able to look at their properties from the Planner's point of view.

The client tries to make the right decision; the seller tries to make a sale. This poses a problem; these outcomes conflict with each other. The sales approach that will help win business is consultative and *helps* the client make a decision. By building a Sales Toolkit that includes Tools of Trust, you ensure a more client-focused approach.

Instead of building a sales process, you build a client-buying process.

I have built a system that, when implemented individually, makes a positive difference at each step, but, when delivered comprehensively, delivers powerful business outcomes. That's when the system delivers maximum results. When you build each step, one by one, you will **WIN** a lot more business.

CIARA FEELY
STEPS
TO WIN

IN THE MEETINGS MARKET

Copyright © 2016 Ciara Feely
STEPS TO WIN

Fisher King Publishing Ltd,
The Studio
Arthington Lane
Pool in Wharfedale
LS21 1JZ
England
www.fisherkingpublishing.co.uk

A CIP catalogue record of this book is available from the British Library
ISBN 978-1-910406-45-8

CONTENTS

Step 1

Stand Out, Sound Different

"Ciara's training in this area will allow hotels and venues to engage in a much more proactive way with clients."

Justine Thomas-Butler, Head of Meetings,
Incentives and Events, Arabian Adventures,
a DMC and PCO Company.

Your Pitch

Stand Out and Sound Different to the Meeting Planner

Like a tree needs roots, a skyscraper needs a solid foundation. To lay the most stable foundation possible for your skyscraper, you must build on bedrock. Decisions in the conference, meeting and event market are based on the solid foundations of proof and trust. We will start building these solid foundations in your Sales Toolkit. I call it the **Conference Converter Toolkit™**; it is what Planners use every day to make their decisions.

Your Sales Toolkit is where Planners start in their venue decision process. You have to get on the list of hotels and venues they will engage with, request a proposal from and with whom they will start a conversation. To do this, we go back to the bedrock and build. That's creating the right pitch, proposal, website and sales and marketing resources that establish trust, confidence and credibility as the right venue for the Planner's event.

I have designed a system to help you attract, convert and **WIN** a lot more group business. It is the **Conference Converter System™**. One of the first steps is to create the right Sales Toolkit for your hotel or venue. These are your Tools of Trust, the tools the Planner uses every day to help make decisions. These are an essential part of the **7 Steps to WIN** in the **Conference Converter System™**.

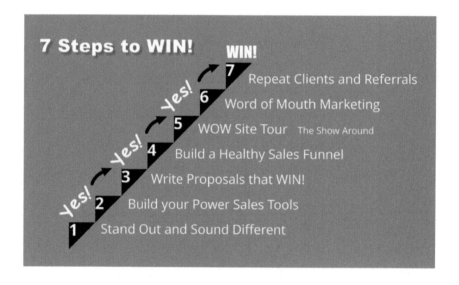

As you can imagine, a big part of the **Conference Converter System™** is building the right toolkit. It makes life easy when you have the right tools for the job. These are sales tools or power sales tools, and I will show you how to build these tools throughout this book.

There are also 7 Ps involved in building this rock solid toolkit, the kind of toolkit that will ensure you attract the right clients and build a level of trust with them so that they are easier to convert. When you attract the right clients, you are in a position to have better quality conversations, conversations that lead to better relationships and relationships that drive revenue.

This is why all sales and conversion systems must start at the very source of the decision-making process. The most common reason that business is lost at more advanced steps in the sales process is through mistakes made at the outset. At these early steps of the sales cycle, you must captivate potential clients and gently pull them closer.

The 7 Steps to WIN!

Clients go through different steps in their decision-making processes. The more **YES**'s you get at each step, the more likely you are to convert the sale. I will break down a few steps of this buying process herein, and show you how to align your sales process with how Planners make decisions. **Aligning how you sell with how the Planner buys will be a key component in dramatically increasing your conversion rate.**

It is a lot more time efficient and profitable to get clients off to a strong start—loving your hotel or venue from the moment they interact with you—on the very first step of their buying process. You want to get to a **YES** at each step of the sales process and keep moving them through each step of their decision-making progression. This is key to your conversion success.

"Strategy gives you direction, but the right tools help you get there more quickly."

The **Conference Converter Toolkit™** is made up of tools that ensure you do the basics brilliantly (the 7 Ps). These are the fundamentals that help you gently pull in and attract the right clients. To quote Chris Brogan, who specializes in helping entrepreneurs build better businesses more quickly: "Every company is looking for *the edge*—what's going to help separate them from their competitors. Well guess what, doing the basics right is *the edge*." I agree with him. It is not complicated. When I ask Planners what frustrates them about looking for a new venue, one (or some) of the following always comes up. These are the 7 Ps, which, when built right, will ensure you do the basics brilliantly.

1. **Power Pitch.** What you say to make the client interested in you. It is not you trying to close the deal.

2. **Position.** Are you positioning yourself as a partner or as a supplier? What you say, and the Sales Toolkits you create, will position you in the marketplace for more wins.

3. **Page.** Your conference webpage and website are vital; they are where up to 60 percent of decision-making happens.

4. **Promise.** This must be built into your marketing resources.

5. **Proposals.** Specifically, proposals that win—with the correct structure, content and pricing options. I have seen as many as 80 percent of leads lost at this step; an excellent proposal changes that dramatically.

6. **Personal.** Proposals have to feel like they were created just for your client and convey that you really understand what they are trying to achieve.

7. **Passion and Personality.** If you are not passionate about your business, why should your Planners be?

"Passion to me is definitely the secret of everything we do."

Ciara Mundrow, Head of International Affairs,
European Society of Cardiology.

The Trust Factor

Serving as a Venue Finder for more than a decade, I noticed a number of factors about the way hotels sell to clients. Many venues fail to build trust and confidence in the right way.

What most industry Sales Toolkits lack is that built-in trust factor. "Trust is the necessary link between a sale and no sale, between how much or how little your client or your next best client spends with you." (I just can't remember who said this, forgive me if it was you.) When Planners book a hotel, they give you their reputation and they place the brand of their organization over your property's brand.

Brands can cost hundreds of thousands of dollars to establish; reputations take years to build. A wrong venue choice can do irreparable damage to both. This fear of reputational loss or brand damage is always there, although it may never be verbalized. Hotels and venues need to include these feelings or emotions of trust, to help Planners overcome their fears and take the next step in their decision-making process.

Trust is the foundation for your new success in attracting and converting more business. I will show you throughout this book how to build trust into each step of your client's decision-making process - your sales process.

Position yourself as a partner instead of being a supplier; it's a lot more lucrative.

Gaining Planner's trust and confidence positions you as their partner instead of their supplier. Being a partner helps you convert business more quickly, and at better rates. In short, it is your fast track to more profitable business.

I teach clients how to gain trust during my online workshops or in-person workshops around the world. It is powerful when the whole team speaks about their property in the same way.

The positioning of your hotel or venue is based on how you develop your pitch and the conversation you have with Planners. If you want to develop this for your property, I've found it is a lot easier to do with a little help. In just one day, you can develop the phrasing that the Conference Planner *wants to hear* in your pitch and *wants to read* on your website and in your sales and marketing brochures. The training exercise that I walk you through is an essential element of your new approach to this market.

The work you are about to do is pivotal to creating a relationship that will transform your position with the Planner from supplier to partner. It is what made the difference for me in my conversations with Planners as a Venue Finder. By immediately demonstrating that I understood their world, I gained Planner's trust quickly, and I got more of their business and stood out from my competition.

A breakthrough in your pitch will help you articulate your position in a way that Planners understand; it will make them sit up and be interested. They will know that you are speaking their language and really "get" them. This approach will help them know that these are the results they want from their conference or event, and you are the only person to help them achieve that. This is what we are going to cover in this first section—the foundation of your new approach to the market. It is vital to spend time thinking about this; creating your unique pitch will reap dividends time after time. Bear in mind, the rest of the steps in this system just won't work in a powerful way if you do not spend the time at this step to get it right.

Stop! Think Like Your Client:

Articulating and communicating how you can help Meeting Planners achieve their goals will make a difference to your sales success—the number of leads you attract and the number of profitable pieces of business you convert and win.

There is a problem in the industry. "Meeting Planners just don't believe the traditional sales pitch by hotel salespeople anymore," says Shawna Suckow, a great industry educator and the founder of SPIN, an association for senior Planners. She sees evidence of it every day in her community of over 3,000 Planners. I am going to show you how to build authentic sales material—material and a message that the Planner does believe.

What's the one thing Planners care about?
Planners do not care about your hotel or venue; they care about their challenges and *the results they want to achieve*. Most

pitches consist of a salesperson talking about their hotel or venue. That is boring, and it all sounds the same. It does not help you stand out, because everyone else is saying the exact same thing.

Planners want an amazing, stress-free event that delivers results.

Planners want to know what you can *do* to help them produce an amazing event (ideally a stress-free one) that achieves the results they want. That is where your sales and marketing efforts should be focused. Sounds simple, right? Well, it is a little more complicated, so I will break it down into simple steps that we can build on.

Start by identifying and valuing the results that you and your venue can help Planners achieve.

You need to talk about your hotel or venue using the words that Meeting Planners identify with. They no longer believe traditional marketing, so the work we do here will help you create "believable" material, material that your target clients will *trust* immediately. You need to create a pitch, and position yourself and your property so that *trust and confidence* occur early in the relationship. Why? Because this will shorten the sales cycle, and help you convert a lot more leads—as well as attract more leads the first place.

This work will be the basis of your conference friendly website, your sales brochure and your proposal, so it's vital to spend your time getting this step of the buying process right. You have to pull in the Planner at this step, so you can smoothly lead them to the next step of their buying process—which is reflected in your sales process.

You will notice I reference this a lot. Converting more business is not about how you want your sales process to be set up, it is knowing and understanding your client's buying process. I don't walk you through how to align those two processes in this book (that might be my next one). I do show private clients how to do so in my online workshops and onsite sales skills days. Clients who aligned their sales process to the buying process tell me it has increased efficiency by as much as 30 percent. It frees up valuable sales time, so you can go after more profitable business that makes a big difference to the bottom line. Hotel owners and General Managers just love it.

The right pitch will help Conference Planners buy, and set you apart from your competition. The work you do on this will be the basis of the stories you tell that Conference Planners will just love; it's real-life material.

What's your pitch or positioning to the Conference Planner? It's what will inspire them to say **YES**, so you must be consistently clear in communicating it.

Your pitch is the *outcome, event objectives or results that you uniquely provide, plus how you do it* (how you provide or deliver this service).

Pitch = Results, Objectives or Outcome + How You Do It

Most pitches focus on the "how." That is, they talk all about the product or service instead of concentrating on the results that the product or service delivers.

What is key here is to spend most of your time talking about the client's **results and outcomes** and a much smaller amount of time speaking about your hotel or venue. That can be hard for most people to do, I know. But it does work. I know from my hotel sales days, I loved my property so much I just wanted to tell everyone about it. Stop! Think about it from your client's point of view. That isn't the most interesting conversation topic for them. Especially at the early stages of their buying process.

You have to build a lot of trust and confidence with them first, before they will listen.

To help you grasp this, take a minute and deliberate. Do you think Planners wake up and say, "I think I will organize a conference in a premier four-star luxury venue that will exceed my expectations?" Or do they wake up thinking about a problem they have—such as needing to sell more products or attract new members—and deciding that running a conference, meeting or event is a way for them to solve that challenge? It's the latter. It's a business decision to organize an event, so a pitch must focus on how you can help Planners achieve business results.

I know it sounds simple. Technically it is. But it can be hard to change the way you sell, especially if you are trying to make that change without any help or guidance. However, most pitches focus on talking about the hotel or venue. You must flip this around and spend most of your time talking about the potential client.

It takes time to switch to this way of thinking and communicating, because we have been doing the opposite for years. Andy Bounds (voted the number one sales trainer in the UK) is the "AFTERs" man. I first heard him speak in 2010 at a BNI

(Business Network International) conference. He focused on this very point—customers want to know how much better off they will be after they have done business with you. They do not buy how you do it. It still took me years to apply this to my business and change the way I communicate with my clients—mainly, because I thought I could do it on my own.

It's hard to be objective about your own pitch and sales approach. Don't make the same mistake I made. From now on think about and speak to your clients from their points of view. Let me help you develop that habit. The quickest way to start getting results from this is to develop the right pitch for your particular property. Remember, the pitch will not be the same for every hotel or venue.

The majority of your pitch must be spent talking about:

Client Outcomes and Event Objectives

For example, most sales presentations talk mainly about a venue's features and benefits—award winning service, number of guestrooms, conference room capacity, number of breakout rooms, location, natural light, delicious food, etc.

What will distinguish you from your competitors, who also have all of this and use it in their main pitches? *Spending the majority of your time focusing on what results you can help Planners achieve*, what outcomes you can help them deliver, what goals and objectives you can help them reach.

Results, outcomes or objectives vary from client to client. You need to master how to determine that for each client. Because unfortunately they don't make it easy and tell you them. It takes time and practice to figure them out. We will get a start on it here. The results you achieve will depend on how much time you put into developing this skill.

Results will vary according to the event. Go back to your existing conference clients and ask them what results you have helped them achieve. Don't worry, I will cover this in the next section on how to gather fantastic testimonials. It is a crucial question to ask your clients.

You cannot completely ignore service delivery; it is, of course, important. Planners must be assured that their events will be the right fit at your venue—that you are not just saying it. You must prove it to them. (Remember, they do not believe traditional sales and marketing pitches). We will cover this, too, a little later in this book.

Suppose that your clients tell you it is much easier to work with you and your team; that is proof for prospective clients. They are listening to that so much more than focusing on the decor of the hotel and how many years' experience your team has. Don't get me wrong, operations are important, but they are not the main focus of your pitch. Everything must flow well during their event, absolutely, but that is not the main area to focus your pitch on. Great service should be a standard; it is not a unique buying proposition.

The Perfect Pitch

"I certainly can relate to everything you are saying and believe you really understand the business when you highlight points about it all being about "YOU" and being passionate. Passion to me, is definitely the secret of everything we do."

Ciara Mundrow,
Head of International Affairs, European Society of Cardiology.

Find the Words to Get Your Clients to Sit Up and Listen

Decision-makers buy and listen based on their event objectives; that is what they pay money for, not how luxurious your property is, or that it fits 300 people.

Moreover, most presentations, at trade exhibitions, on venue websites and in marketing material, focus on the wrong things. People start selling service delivery, location or features and benefits! An effective pitch must be results- and objectives-focused.

As a Venue Finder, I have had many salespeople whip out the photos right away and start talking about their hotel or venue. That is not what interests me at this step in my buying process. It's not going to make me recommend the hotel or know if it is a match for any particular conference. I am usually bored after five minutes. You have to take the time to sit back and really understand the Conference Planner's needs. You must focus on what they want to accomplish with their conference, because that is what helps you know what your pitch should be.

So, when you change the conversation with a Planner to be results focused and all about them, you have a conversation that your *target market wants to hear* and to which they are attentively listening!

For example, when I present my "How to a Build a WOW Toolkit Workshop," I focus on the results for the sales and operations teams. I focus on the results for the team that can help them generate more leads that are easier to convert.

I spend more of my time talking about:

- Outcomes similar clients have achieved, such as increasing conversion rates by 30%
- Growing profits and market share
- Shifting a hotels ranking in the STAR report
- Increasing sales productivity

as that is what General Managers want to hear.

I ran this workshop recently at a client's hotel with both the sales and operations teams. They converted a new piece of business worth $250,000 within four weeks of completing the workshop. That is so much more appealing than me telling you I run sales training workshops, it's a two-hour session, we have fun team-building exercises and everyone walks away understanding Planners and their needs. It gets implemented more quickly, as you have both operations and sales agreeing to take certain actions together.

So, we want to come up with a host of words that will position you as a leader in the sales conversation—words that will result in Planners calling you, wanting to book and importantly not focusing on the rate. That is the double advantage to taking this approach. That is the beauty of it.

To be clear; we are not developing an elevator pitch or snappy tagline. What I help people understand is how to make clients interested. With a series of exercises, I show hotel and venue sales teams how to be leaders in the sales process and guide clients to say **YES** and buy from you. That is a very different position to develop with your client. It is a lot more powerful, as it develops profitable relationships with your Planner's best outcomes at the heart of the process.

Some of the most overused words I hear in hotel pitches are phrases such as "exceeding expectations," "great location," "family run" and "successful event." What you must remember is that your competition is also saying "exceeding expectations," "great location," "family run" and "successful event." You must stand out from your competition and appeal to the emotions of the Meeting Planner by using more effective words and phrases.

Why Does All of This Matter?

Working on your pitch involves finding a whole range of words that resonate with your clients. Use the *words that come right out of your client's mouth*. These words are already circulating in their heads. When you find these words, you can plug them into any of my other programs such as "Building a Healthy Sales Funnel" and "How to do a WOW Site Tour" (because there is no point in doing an average one anymore).

I have spent a lot of time getting into my own client's heads. This gives me the foundation of my sales conversation, my website and my marketing resources. What I have found, though, is I just couldn't do it on my own. I needed someone who was not in my business to bounce off of. What I was coming up with just wasn't effective. So I got help. I decided to redo all of my marketing, which was a hard decision to make. However, it was so worth it. My conversion rate skyrocketed. Since then, I can be selective about who I market to or with whom I invest my time speaking. With my new marketing and new pitch, hoteliers say to me, "Ciara, it is like you read my mind." That is the effect your words and your Sales Toolkit should have on prospective clients.

Now, I want to show you how to use the words your clients say to create other materials, such as your presentations, your website, your marketing materials and your social media. These words and phrases are brilliant blog material and help attract qualified traffic to your website—more business that is easier to convert! They love what you wrote on your blog or in your sales brochure, and they call you—already half converted—because you use the right words. The words your ideal clients use will also help you create sales and opt-in pages that Planners will click on.

The words we come up with are words that will resonate with your perfect clients. They will not resonate with people who are not your ideal clients. You cannot convert every Conference and Meeting Planner, so you might as well concentrate on the ones that you can!

You want to work with 100 percent of the Planners that are yours to help *and* convert, of course. It could save you 80 percent of your time. There are a lot of hotels and venues out there wasting 80 percent of their time going after leads and sending out proposals for business that they will never convert; we have all experienced the time-wasters. You want to avoid that situation at all costs, because it is very common in the industry and it ultimately costs hundreds of thousands in wasted sales opportunities. Finding the right words helps you find more of your perfect clients.

Great salespeople and marketers phrase their sales materials the way their clients phrase things. Great pitches are filled with the words your client's use; they speak the client's language. Planners will feel that you get them. Great marketing tells a story, and we are searching for your client's stories. Why?

Because that is what Planners believe in.

Listen for phrases that are already ringing in your ideal client's ears. That is going to attract them. That is going to get the phone ringing. That is going to take the focus off rate.

These words are powerful and communicate your value in your verbal and written materials—your proposal, your website, your sales brochure, your social media. These are words that will drive revenue.

Action Items from This Section:

- Observe the language your clients use. Write it down.

- If you would like help to find the right words, the language of your clients, connect with me and we can explore a few options as to how I can help you.

www.ConferenceConverter.com/connect

What are my top learnings so far?

WONDERFUL
OPPORTUNITY
TO WIN

WOW

Space Communicates A Message

"We are always trying to get an edge, trying to figure out how to make Meeting Planners happy and win their repeat business. I really want to know their hot buttons. This is great because we get to learn what drives them nuts. We came up with a game plan and some bullet points, some great things to apply with the team in Texas."

David Townsend, Director of Conference & Convention Planning, San Louise Resort, Galveston Convention Center, Texas, USA.

When I speak about positioning in the marketplace, I refer to how the Planner views your team, hotel or venue. Judgments are made on a number of different criteria. I have talked about the pitch so far. Creating the right Sales Toolkit will also help you position yourself as a partner for Meeting Planners.

There is a wonderful realization happening in the industry right now, and that is how space itself and meeting design can influence the outcomes of an event. I find the topic fascinating. In this section, I will share with you facts, opinions and experiences from a host of people I interviewed on this topic.

Space design has a massive effect on the outcome and results of a conference or meeting. It affects:

- People's mood.

- How easy it is for them to meet people.

- Their absorption of information.

- How well they retain and recall information.

- The overall emotional experience they have at the conference—what they will remember and talk about.

- What they walk away thinking and saying about the hotel or venue.

- Most of all *if they will recommend* the hotel venue or, indeed, *the conference to their connections*.

In writing this section, I spoke with many "Space Architects," meeting designers, communications experts, hotel architects and interior designers. I also interviewed Hotel Directors, such as Ted Brumleve of Dolce Hotels and Simon Turner of Starwood, and Conference Planners to ensure I had practical "implementable" suggestions that work and had a revenue model behind them.

Fiona McDonald of Spatial Design Limited, Cork, Ireland, said something to me that struck home: "Space communicates a message." Fiona's thoughts and writings formed the basis of this whole section and thought spectrum. She is quoted many times throughout this section. The challenge for us is to ensure the venue is helping the Planners to communicate the right message to meeting participants. It must help them to achieve the big aim of every gathering—for people to connect, meet and feel comfortable in their environment.

Design Impacts the Outcome

This section will help you see how important it is to talk about the layout of the meeting space and, most importantly, how that can impact the success of a conference.

Spending time, walking through networking space with the Planner is vital to converting more conference business. If you are up to date and can help educate the Conference Planner on how the space can be utilized to help delegates get more from their conference experience, then you are speaking their language and profiling yourself as an important partner on their conference team.

Space helps to deliver a message with impact. To quote Fiona McDonald: "It has three functions at a conference, meeting or event."

1. To **facilitate** networking, and enable individuals to interact with each other in smaller groupings. The right design of space can make the initial meeting easier and help people to converse and strike up conversations.

2. To **enhance** networking by incorporating spaces that are more isolated and more comfortable so that people can step away, have more private conversations and develop their relationships. This is where the real business is done, and opportunities develop further.

3. To **influence** and help participants retain, recall and implement the knowledge they have learned *after* they leave. This is the dream of every Conference Planner. If your hotel or venue can influence this, and you are speaking about this as part of your pitch, then conversion rates will soar.

According to Fiona McDonald: "Creating the right space for networking is more relevant and critical now than ever before." The challenge for designers is to ensure that the space itself serves to generate network formation and connections with new people.

Designers must, therefore, maximize the opportunity for individuals to spend time together for the purpose of interaction. They must also maximize the opportunity to intensify the experience of that potential interaction at an emotional level that further encourages engagement.

Engagement is a big buzz word in the industry. It is one of the major challenges Conference and Meeting Planners have - how to get participants to engage and participate in an event.

There is a psychology behind well-thought out space.

Communication experts spend hours and days observing how people use existing space and what walk patterns they use. To really get it right, collaboration between the architect, designer, communications expert and Conference Organizers brings a more holistic approach to creating multi-functional space. The introduction of this approach can hugely impact networking space success.

What Are the Must-Haves of Venue Design?

Here are the top "must-haves" of conference- and meeting-friendly design of venue space.

1. **Natural Light** is fantastic to have in the conference room. It is "golden" in the networking area, according to Ted Brumleve. It not only affects people's mood and how comfortable they feel, but it also influences their conversation; at the very least, people have the weather to talk about.

2. **Moveable furniture** and plants will influence the direction people walk in and where they congregate. It will influence how easy it is to strike up a spontaneous conversation, according to Fiona McDonald. Niki Schafer, a UK Interior Designer, attended a networking event in London recently; she emailed me after the event with this practical comment.

"Open spaces are awful for networking. Cliques form easily, and there's no flow to ensure people move on." Have you ever got "stuck" talking to the same person at an event?

3. **Network, Atmosphere and Ambiance** is essential in facilitating networking and sharing of information. Ciara Mundrow told me she spends considerable money creating coffee shops and lounges at their events for medical professionals. Delegates want spaces where they can be social. Ben Goedegebuure, Global General Manager of EMEA Maritz Travel said: "The most valuable space in a venue is space where people can sit and have conversations. The networking space is critical."

4. **Flexibility of space** is one of the key attributes Simon Turner's team looks for. "Having space left wide open a number of days a week is an investor turn off. Space must be adaptable, efficient and sub-divisible, so it can be offered in many different forms and incarnations. Return on investment for a hotel owner is meaningfully driven by facilities design."

5. **"There must be balance struck between neutral space and characterful space,"** says James Dilley of Jestico + Whiles. Hotel companies now want universal space that is flexible. Art exhibitions, conferences, weddings and parties all have different design needs. The sales team does not want to be held back by past design. It needs to be able to say **YES**, and be able to adapt the space easily. The problem or challenge this creates for the design team is that meeting this brief can create bland spaces.

6. **Great lighting** affects the mood. Consider this tip from Ted Brumleve: "Invest in a lighting expert at the design stage, as how a room is lit affects people's moods at events." Day lighting, soft lighting that makes everyone look good, evening lighting and night-time lighting all play their individual roles in the successful outcome of an event.

7. **Brilliant technology** behind the scenes is crucial. Hoteliers Ted Brumleve and Simon Turner say conference centers and meeting places must be wired to help the Meeting Planner run smooth events. There is no excuse for delegates complaining about the strength of the Wi-Fi, quality of the projection or not being able to see the presentations clearly. Technology is a vital aspect of design to help future-proof a hotel or venue. When renovating or creating space, wire it for more than just today's technology so that it is easy to add new innovations as technology advances and the venue's needs change.

8. **Ensure there is access to outside**, says Richard Penner of Cornell University. Offer patios near the networking areas, as delegates need to get a sense of where they are and the environment they are in during break times. They need to be able to revitalize. The feeling of being cooped up and indoors all day affects delegates' abilities to absorb and retain information.

9. **Event space must entertain**. Planners need the space to make an impact; when delegates walk into a venue that's different, there is an immediate effect. Offer "something really cool, something that is visual, that stimulates the senses," says Ben Goedegebuure of Maritz Travel, one of the world's largest and most established Venue Finders. It

gives people something to comment on and helps them start conversations with complete strangers. That makes networking a whole lot easier!

10. **Consider a sense of location** that it is not generic (tip from Amy Jakubowski of Wilson Associates, Los Angeles). Space should communicate and reflect its location. Leave attendees with an unmistakable sense of where they are. They should not feel that they could be at any venue, anywhere in the world. People want to be entertained by how a building looks and the environment around them. It enhances the experiences of conference participants and helps make an event more memorable. Great examples of buildings that give you a sense of location include The Dublin Convention Centre in Ireland with five floors of glass walls looking out over Dublin Bay and the city or Ballymaloe Grainstore in Cork, Ireland, a converted grain store that has a rustic, relaxed yet professional feel to it.

11. **"Space must offer convenience,"** according to Ben Goedegebuure. People want to experience convenience. The conference delegate wants to experience their lives in venues, having access to Wi-Fi is important because it allows them to work and continue with their days outside of the event. Delegates wants as much convenience as possible, so they are not stressed about what they are missing at home or in their professional lives.

Conference attendees today want authenticity—a sense of place they can make their own.

Design and Impact

Planners are changing how they run conferences and events. Meeting architecture has seriously advanced in the last few years. How delegates want to participate in a conference has also changed dramatically. They want more involvement and a say in topics discussed.

The space outside the conference room is just as important to the success of an event as the conference room itself. Ted Brumleve of Dolce Hotels calls this space the Town Hall of the conference. **It is the connector to the rest of the hotel, and it is where people meet and make connections.**

Delegates gather in the space outside conference rooms and get away from the information fed to them throughout an event. They take a breath, and hit the refresh button.

In particular, millennials may not want to participate in a conference in the traditional way; they will take breaks when they feel like it. Dolce Hotels is changing the food and beverage delivery to meet this demand; refreshments are available all day. Richard Maxfield of Dolce says they have created *Nourishment Hubs* so conference participants can graze and feel more at home.

"Meetings continue beyond the meeting room, and the venue set up and layout must facilitate this."

This is a major way that venues can help the Conference Planner get bigger, more powerful results from their conferences by facilitating new spaces for networking.

Your Space Must Match Planner Needs

You need to sell your space to match what the Planner is buying.

Furniture placement and the design of a space influences how people socialize and move around. According to Fiona McDonald, "Well-spaced seating arrangements and private conversation hubs will greatly enhance the networking and business relationships formed at an event." Venues should design their spaces to facilitate these relationships to help the Conference Planner deliver more effective and productive networking. One reason people attend events is to network, so speaking about your space in terms of the results it achieves is key. Taking this angle in your pitch gives you a big competitive advantage.

Space Design and Networking

By Fiona McDonald of Spatial Design Limited, Cork, Ireland;
Contributing Author.

The designer could choose to assign the arrangement of space
for networking purposes in a way that is conducive to individuals
interacting with each other in smaller groups. The designer may
also incorporate spaces that are more isolated, that provide
space with more privacy off the main areas, which may be
more effective in furthering existing relationships or provide for
undisturbed discussion. This space helps to facilitate the real
business happening at a conference. This can seriously impact
people's decision to return to the venue and make it an annual
event.

This is a rather simplistic example of how designers may begin
to think about space. However, it illuminates the point that
space itself is the single most effective means of going about
constructing the architecture of facilitating networking.

The designer's job is to ensure the precise requirement of the
client and user are met. To that end, another factor that would
surely influence the design of network space is if participants, as

a result of the design, were to retain, recall and implement the knowledge they have learned after they have left the space. This "effect" can be achieved through thoughtful design.

Space Design Influences Learning

Space can be designed to "consider how knowledge is transferred, which means, how individuals integrate prior knowledge with new knowledge, and how they subsequently disseminate it," according to Fiona McDonald.

Spaces influence how individuals internalize the content of messaging before they leave. If they internalize the content, it can be better retained, better recalled and better implemented or repeated after the event.

If a venue can show that conference participants retain and learn more because of the way their space is set up, it could show Planners how to overcome a big challenge. In the next section, I will give you some practical examples of space design and its impact on delegates, as shared by Helen Kuyper in the section on how the role of the sales professional is evolving.

Emotions and Tactility
By Ann Hansen of Concept + Competence, Denmark; Contributing Author.

Meetings very often communicate content using only words and visuals. When elements are introduced to a meeting that you can touch, feel and create with your hands, another dimension is achieved. In combination with spoken words and visuals, a whole other learning experience is created. That is because this interaction connects us with our emotions and the spin-off of this is that participants will remember more and be able to apply it quicker to their work or life.

The idea is to make something that is intangible tangible. One idea to achieve this is to integrate themed props and physical items into the room design.

When we use our hand's something new happens. Another sense of meaning and understanding of a topic will emerge when we create something together. "Playing" socially "bonds" together participants; the physical and tangible, allows conversations and creativity which flow in a much more natural way.

I experienced this myself with Ann and her business partner Bo Krüger who designed and facilitated the MPI EMEC Conference in 2015. It was an event full of interaction, play, creating and connecting with complete strangers. I knew two people walking into the room of 400 people. I made meaningful connections and learned and applied my learning within a few days of the conference. I still recall elements, because of the playful way I learned and it makes application of these ideas a lot easier.

The Happiness Factor

Natural Light, the Happiness Factor and Helping the Planner to Say YES

"When people are happy, they have more dopamine in their system. Dopamine turns on every learning center in the human brain."

Source: The Happiness Advantage by Shawn Achor

"The amount and wavelength of light affect the different functions of the brain, including the regulation of a person's thoughts and feelings. With this knowledge comes a realization that simple adjustments in lighting in homes and workspaces can make a lot of difference to the way a person thinks and feels."

Source: examinedexistence.com

When your conversation with the Planner is centered on helping them to achieve two of the big reasons people attend conferences:

1. To make connections.
2. To learn.

Then you have the Planners attention. The team must talk about the hotel or venue's facilities in that way, from that angle to help the Planner to say **YES**.

In many pitches I hear from hotels and venues, they refer to their great location, or simply that they have natural light in the main meeting space area. These are being quoted as USPs and reasons for Planners to book with them. However, I feel they are very much selling themselves short. Not only are they sounding like every other hotel out there who can say the same thing. They are missing out on a big emotional factor that would immediately influence a decision in their favor.

When we as human beings are positive, our brains become more engaged, creative, motivated, energetic, resilient and productive.

These are all emotions most Planners want their delegates experiencing at an event. If a venue has natural light in the meeting space area, then it is helping to create happier meeting attendees. This is a much stronger pitch than simply stating you have natural light.

If a hotel sales team is having this level of discussion with a Planner, they are immediately positioning themselves to be of more value to the Planners outcomes. It is a great conversation to have when on a hotel tour. Time should be spent in the space to help the Planner process these facts and feel the effects themselves. This type of conversation enables the sales team to speak directly to the part of the Planner's brain that makes decisions. Why? Because this is an emotional outcome, the Planner wants to get from the conference. It would be solving one of their big problems – helping delegates to implement what they learned at the conference to ensure lasting change.

Natural Light

Natural Light affects how the brain absorbs and retains information.

In my Venue Finding days, while on a site tour, I found most sales pitches consisted of walking into the conference room and the sales person pointing out that there is natural light in the room.

That is an opportunity missed, that is stopping short of what the Planner needs to hear to make a **YES** decision. Continuing the conversation to talk about the benefits of natural light and the results it can help the Planner to achieve such as improved learning and ability of the delegate to listen and retain what they are communicating at the conference, is what the Planner needs to hear in order to book with you. Why? Because it is helping to solve a major challenge they have in running their events. It is so much more powerful than just saying: "we have natural light in the meeting room." It is speaking to the core of one of their main problems.

"Having natural light in a conference room is a blessing," according to Ted Brumleve. "It can change the mood and can temper the spirit." However, what do you do if your venue does not have natural light in the main conference room? Here are a few ideas from the experts:

- Lighting Technology. Ensure the ability to adjust lighting. Have varying texture and volume of lighting on the floor, wall and ceiling. Fuse a mix of lighting types - incandescent, fluorescent, LED. In the section on creating your Tech Toolkit, I share with you tips from Brandt Krueger on how to use projection mapping to create amazing lighting effects that impact the outcome of a conference or event.

- Strategically place mirrors to reflect light and give an illusion of natural light. Mirrors can be shaped to look like windows and help create this effect.

- Bring the outside in, change the color scheme to reflect the outside – natural shades of green, woody browns, stone grey, and soft pallet tones of neutral color. Make people at least feel like they are outside even if they cannot see out! Amy Jakubowski of Wilson Associates made this suggestion along with the idea to create texture in a room, so the walls are not just flat and plain. Use carpet design and wall design to make people feel like they are walking outside.

- Put photos on the wall of your space. Large, panoramic prints so people can feel like they are looking at a beautiful mountain scene, seascape or cityscape. Create the illusion of a window as if it is the view they are looking out on. You could even frame it with curtains. I saw this idea in the Inspirational Hotel of the Future at the Best Western Members Conference.

"Design is a serious business," according to Fiona McDonald. There must be an analytical, evidence-based approach overlaying the creative dynamics of good design processes to help make great design decisions. There is a good deal of sense in promoting partnerships with other design professionals, in particular, creative communications agencies. However, it's important to include marketing strategists, graphic designers, architectural landscapers, in-house Floor Managers and Conference Planners in the design process also. Understanding how space influences human behavior is a fundamental and evidence-informed approach to satisfying the client and the venue supplier provision.

Space is the largest capital acquisition a business will most likely make, and therefore, the designer's responsibility is to protect and maximize its potential value by protecting and maximizing its effects on individuals. This is the key to capitalizing on and controlling that value.

Space Communicates a Message

Space always delivers a message but delivering the right message calls for carefully considered design discussion. The link between design and having space that is very "Sellable," taking space from design concept to the reality of selling the space.

James Dilley of Jestico + Whiles makes a great point that because hotel design now has to be flexible and adaptable to be able to host a meeting, fashion show or funeral. This can lead to bland, neutral space that doesn't have a lot of pizzazz and character. This kind of space is harder to market. Photography is key, in this case, to selling the space to different markets and making it easy for each client-type to picture their event there. James points out that much preliminary searching for a venue is done online and the first impression comes from thumbnail photos, so the designer almost has to be designing for websites and how space will look in a picture on the internet as well as the reality of the physical appearance.

This is a dimension that didn't exist for design until recently. Marketers need to understand the reality of selling space and cyber selling, making that first impression online. How a room is set up for different occasions and photographed is what is key here. The space has to be able to fit any booking; conference, motorbike launch, party or team-build so the design methodology may end up being a vanilla approach.

Using technology such as media walls, projection mapping, and lighting is a possible solution here for the marketer. James makes a brilliant point that the images online have to have power and energy to them; this is a modern phenomenon to hotel marketing.

Spaces are no longer designed as sealed boxes. Hotels and venues will now use any space for functions, which gives a flow effect to them, rather than just putting everyone in a conference room. Sliding doors and glass walls are some of the design techniques used to help create this type of space rather than just a conference box.

There is a big demand out there for unusual venues and as James puts it "a spirited place." Atmosphere is key to any event. Paul O'Mahony of @omaniblog is someone I have had many fascinating discussions with about the topic of venues and what role they play in the outcome of an event. He makes a very valid point that in the invitation to an event, people immediately look to see where it is being held. They make an assumption about the event based on the type of venue it is being held in. It is one of the first main messages being communicated about the kind of event it will be; a standard conference in a standard venue or a WOW venue which would mean it will be a WOW event.

"Events are now held in a Tower Bridge or a Garden, the challenge for the venue designer is to bring an element of a 'spirited place' into hotel and venue design, from rooms to lobby to function space. It used to be that universality was the goal."

James Dilley of Jestico + Whiles

The "cookie cutter" style is what I remember referring to it as in the late 90s, in my early hotel sales days. All the big brands were designed that way in America, so the American traveler felt a sense of familiarity traveling internationally. Now the Marriott in New York does not have to look like the one in London or Shanghai, according to Amy Jakubowski of Wilson Associates, Los Angeles. Hotels need to tell their story, need to differentiate and how that is communicated to the Planner has a big impact on the types of events they win.

Planner Problems
The 3pm Slump and How to Overcome It

How Air Quality affects the participation of attendees at a Conference

A Planner shared with me recently that she cut a meeting short by 1.5 hours because of the space. The room was too warm, and there was no way she could work with people in that environment. The venue did not generate repeat business from this Planner or positive word of mouth. Sales teams do not always pay attention to how an event is run on the day. It is, however, a very important part of their ability to generate repeat business and word of mouth marketing. Air quality plays an important role in this, however, it is rarely talked about.

An abstract published in the US Natural Library of Medicine showed that productivity is increased by 15 percent once pollutants were removed from the air. The reason why indoor air quality is hugely important to the conference space and meeting rooms is to provide an environment where clients feel energized being in the space. The Meeting Planner wants the delegates to come back for day two and tell their friends and colleagues about the great experience they had at the event.

How energized the participants feel hugely affects their ability to network and network productively. Inspiring conversations cannot be sparked if attendees feel like they are in a slump and just want to get out of the space. I had that feeling at a conference I attended recently. I left thinking I did not want to go back to it next year (and I didn't!). The air was stagnant, there was no natural light in the room or the networking area, apart from a small skylight that I found myself trying to stand under all the time. I had an urge to leave the networking area at each break and walk towards the light.

When negative emotions are felt by delegates at an event, no matter how brilliant the speakers are or delicious the food is, it will affect the overall feedback participants give to the Conference Organizer. Sometimes it may be the main topic they talk about and their overall memory of the event. The venue plays a large part in avoiding those experiences for conference participants and ensuring repeat business and positive word of mouth.

No matter how good the event space is and what technology

or mod cons are in it, if clients become drowsy and can't concentrate during the day and want to leave after lunch, a huge opportunity has been missed. Some people even develop a headache.

The following few paragraphs are important to share with the operations team. When a room is filled with people, carbon dioxide and moisture levels start building. After one single hour people become affected, two hours in people get drowsy, three hours in people just are not able to concentrate no matter how interesting or funny the speaker is.

Air Quality Tech

By Michael Cahalane, Passive House Consultant and Builder; Contributing Author.

The environment in a conference room changes rapidly once it is full of people. People in the room will breathe from 0.5 to 2m3 air per hour (APH) and will emit from 0.02 to 0.08m3 per hour of carbon dioxide. With one hundred people in a room, before lunch-time the room will be at 8 to 32m3 per hour and the effect is that they cannot concentrate. In effect, they are being partially poisoned.

The temperature levels also rise quickly to uncomfortable levels if the air is not constantly being changed.

There are some easy solutions to this that don't involve knocking down walls. To eliminate complaints about air quality, CO_2 levels should not exceed 1000 parts per million. (A person requires 30m³ / hour of air supply). A solution to this is to place sensors in the room and monitor them throughout the day, the results should not exceed 1000 PPM, this rate varies from country to country. The WSU Energy Program is a good guideline to reference more information on this.

To ensure enough oxygen to everyone in the room, it is necessary to ensure enough air changes per hour. The heating also needs to be balanced with the correct air supply in the room. This may sound complicated, it is not. The sensors can be connected to a smart controller to monitor and respond to carbon dioxide levels; just like it responds to a thermostat setting for temperature.

This may sound like it will cost a fortune – look at it as an investment. There are additional benefits when the space is designed properly. The following can be achieved:

- Filters on the air system remove pollen for hay fever sufferers, Legionnaire's disease (caused by warm water pools in the air conditioning systems, bacteria grow in these pans) and mold. Conference Planners are hearing more and more about both, before and after a conference, from allergy sufferers. If they can immediately say they have considered this and chosen a venue that has filters to remove these, then it goes a long way in helping them secure more bookings and maintain a positive image for their brand and reputation.

- Correct air changes per hour (ACH) supplies oxygen and removes CO_2, CO, Volatile organic compounds, moisture, and ozone. These are required standards by many educational facilities and in the UK, schools must have 2.5 ACH. Can your operations team tell you what your ACH is?

- Silencers are part of these heat recovery systems and sound like a whisper at 25 dB.

.

A very simple way to assure the Planner that you have thought through the issue of air quality is to purchase carbon dioxide monitors (from $200 plus). Your operations team should monitor it throughout the day. Refreshing the room with fresh air at lunch-time and break times is a quick and easy fix to this problem.

Air Quality Solutions

There are Air Quality Systems that help to overcome this problem.

A Passive Heating and Cooling System is a more natural way to ensure a better air quality and help keep delegates engaged and alert. A Passive Heating and Cooling system ensures:

- Better air quality and it is more cost effective.

- More attentive attendees as better air quality keeps the brain more alert.

- An overall better experience at the conference when our physical space is optimized for the body's peak performance.

Being able to have this level of conversation with the Planner helps position yourself as an expert in your area. Being considered a trusted advisor in how your venue can help Planners deliver the kind of results they want to achieve at your venue, it will help you to win a lot more business and be considered a partner, rather than a supplier.

Action Items from This Section:

- Share this section with your operations department. They have to realize the effect their work can have on your clients.

- There are wonderful people in the industry that I work with, that can help develop your whole team to contribute to your client's event in this way. Educating your clients on an even better way to run their event is a sure way to position your team as being of high value to them. This is the future of events. Conferences will not continue to be delivered in the usual lecture style, theatre or classroom set-ups. Connect with me if you would like to discuss ideas on this.

www.ConferenceConverter.com/connect

What are my top learnings so far?

WONDERFUL
OPPORTUNITY
TO WIN

WOW

Step 2

Build Your Sales Toolkit

"We have converted a two-year deal for monthly training worth £250,000 to our hotel. It's directly as a result of the approach Ciara taught the team."

Danielle Isles, Director of Sales,
Weetwood Hall Hotel and Conference Centre, Leeds, UK.

"Strategy gives you direction, but the right tools help you get there quicker."

How to Change a Planner's Mind

The inspiration for what I am about to share came from a book given to me by Rick Armstrong of Fisher King Publishing. It helped me articulate a point that I could feel in my bones, but couldn't express to Conference Organizers or venues. So, thank you, Rick, for sending me *More Time to Think* by Nancy Kline, not the singer (I am a big fan of both). When I received it from Rick, I thought, when will I ever get time to read this? My boys were just turning two at the time, and they were full-on! But I did find the time to read it, and was struck by the section "Space to Think." It helped me perfect my pitch to Conference Organizers and for them to see the value in what I do as a Venue Finder. It articulated the value of getting the venue right, and how that affects the thinking and creativity results of an event.

The essence of the section is this: **People think better when the space around them says, "You matter."** If you need the outcome of a meeting, conference or team-build to be new fresh thinking, creative input/output or a new perspective, then ensuring that the venue allows for this, that the environment, surroundings and atmosphere are right, will greatly help deliver a more productive event. I go into a lot more detail on this in the section "How Space Communicates a Message."

Atmosphere is key to any event. It is that *something* about a meeting or conference that you won't know you got wrong until it is too late. Hotels and venues rarely speak about it, but it is an essential element of any event. It sets the tone. It is something you can feel the minute you walk in the door.

Derek Reilly, a BNI colleague and Area Managing Director for Ireland West, asked me to help him find the right venue for a JCI (Junior Chamber International) conference he organized. He said he never really understood what I did (as a Venue Finder) until I asked him the *right questions about the outcome he wanted from his conference.* This is how the sequence of events went. He was the newly appointed president of JCI in the west of Ireland. It was his first time to organize this particular conference, but he had attended previous events.

He called me and asked me to book X Hotel for his conference. That was the one he wanted, and he was quite set on that. He asked me to do the negotiating and ensure everything went right. I never had such an easy request before. However, I knew the hotel he had chosen, and I needed to ensure for myself that it was the right one. So, I asked him a few questions about his conference.

- **What was the No. 1 result he wanted to get from the conference?** The answer was networking. It was paramount. It was an annual event, and the majority of the delegates only met this one time a year. As an organization, they needed to work together remotely, so friendships built at the conference needed to sustain this.

The other powerful question I asked him was…

- **What would you change about last year's conference?**
  He thought hard about this one. He said that because it
  had been held in a popular small city, everyone went off in
  different groups, in different directions, out on the town
  for the night. It proved to be impossible to keep everyone
  together on both the Friday and Saturday night of the event.

Consider the differences the right venue can make to the outcome of an event.

In essence, the networking element of the conference, a main
outcome of the event, was severely diluted as a result of the
conference location and the chosen venue. This is a major issue
for many Planners, and choosing a venue that makes it easy for
everyone to walk off, will just compound the problem.

The better quality questions you ask; the better quality answers you get.

Based on the two answers Derek gave me to two questions, I
knew he had chosen the wrong hotel for his convention. On his
next site inspection, I asked him to please go to Y Hotel, which I
felt was the right venue for his conference. How did I know this?

- It was 1.5 miles out of town, so it was a little bit harder for
  people to go to the pubs in town. (The hotel he had chosen
  was right in the town center, and everyone would have
  disappeared the minute they checked in.)

- It was a smaller hotel, and his conference would be the
  only event taking place there that weekend; essentially, it
  became their hotel. The hotel Derek originally chose was

much bigger and had a wedding and one other big event happening that same weekend.

Going with the smaller hotel meant that they had the staff's full attention; everything the hotel did that weekend was for his conference delegates alone. The delegates felt special, and that made life much easier for him.

Derek did a site inspection at both properties and called me the minute he left the hotel I recommended. He said: "Ciara, you are right, Y Hotel is the right venue for my conference, I can see that now." He made the booking and the conference was the most successful in its ten-year history. He said: "It raised the bar for every other convention." I followed the conference on Facebook that weekend, and I could just feel the atmosphere.

It was electric. The feedback on the venue and conference was fantastic. Derek now understood what I did as a Venue Finder; he understood the difference getting the location and venue right made to the conference. Not one delegate left the hotel that weekend, which was a first. The networking was powerful, as he had a captive audience. Derek looked great in the eyes of his peers (which was important to him as an outcome). He also experienced another transformation in his life as a result. He was rightly nominated to the European Council of JCI that year. The success of the conference had seriously helped catapult his profile within the organization. Another great outcome.

There is an opportunity to convert leads by asking Planners the right questions. I go into a lot detail on how to do this in the "15 Killer Questions" I developed, which I share with my online program participants. It takes time to develop the right questions for your market, your property and your specific clients. It then takes a little more time and practice to develop confidence in implementing this sales technique. Change doesn't happen instantly. What the industry has to get away from is just asking about dates, rates and space.

By asking brilliant questions, you can get essential information on how your venue can help Planners achieve their desired results. It takes the conversation away from rate.

You may find that Planners have not considered every aspect of their events beforehand. Derek never made the connection between the location of his conference venue and the problem he had with keeping people together for networking. He assumed there was nothing he could do about this annual problem. Asking Derek the right questions and matching aspects of the venue as a solution, helped him see that it could be fixed.

Some Planners are organizing conferences for the first time and haven't yet learned this valuable lesson.

It's an area in which venues can help educate Planners on the value of choosing the right venue and the difference that can make to their events. The sales team, however, must position itself as the expert in the space—consult with clients on how it can help them achieve their desired results, in order to attract and convert more leads.

Avoid Being Seen as A Commodity by The Planner

Crafting your Sales Toolkit and a pitch that helps your venue to stand out is the best way to ensure you are not viewed as a commodity, just another hotel or venue, which is the same as any other venue in the Planners eyes.

I regularly hear from salespeople all over the world, in every market, that they struggle to get the conversation away from the rate. They feel the business is lost over rate or they end up negotiating with the Planner to the point that their profits are eroded. There is much frustration around this issue, not just with salespeople but with GMs and owners too. Moreover, I hear you. I had this problem in my hotel sales days in San Francisco. The rate is important; it is part of the Planners job to get great rates. Some Planners have even taken training on how to negotiate rates. So it must be handled in a certain way.

In my ten years as a Venue Finder, no client ever came to me and asked me to find the cheapest venue. When I applied a questioning technique that I have developed (I call them my *Killer Questions*), I was able to uncover what their very hot buying buttons were. The rate was in the top five list of priorities, but it was rarely their number one. Anyone can quote rates; it does not take skill to lower rates. If selling your meeting space and guestrooms at the cheapest rates is your strategy, then this book will not help you. However, if you want to be in the top percentage of salespeople in your industry, then that takes mastery and knowing how to take the focus off the rate.

It is key to remember when dealing with this market that

reputations and brands are at stake. Reputations take years to develop; brands cost hundreds of thousands to build. A wrong venue choice can do serious damage to both. That is why, at the beginning steps of the client's buying process, it is so important to build the right level of trust and confidence with the Planner.

You then need to be consistent in building that trust and confidence factor with the Planner. We do this by seamlessly building it into our Sales Toolkit. Why? Because that is what Planners use every day to help them make their decisions.

Your Sales Toolkit is what Planners use every day to help them make a decision.

Let's start with taking a look at the language that is very common in the industry. This is the language that is intended to make the Planner want to choose a particular hotel or venue. I have come up with a list of words that *do not* inspire confidence. I have put together a list of the most overused words in the industry. Words and phrases that make a venue sound the same as every other hotel or venue out there. Avoid the following phrases if you want to distinguish your venue:

- Premier venue, Memorable Experience, Relax and unwind, Ideal venue...
- Family run
- State of the art facilities
- Perfect venue for X – then listing ten different types of events some venues even have weddings thrown in. (Avoid at all costs mentioning weddings in your Sales Toolkits)
- Perfect space for any event – conference, meeting

exhibition, any size, large or small. This is too general! Don't just list every type of event you can think of. Give each one a short paragraph and say why the space suits this type of event. If an organizer is organizing X type of event, they will just skip to that description.

I have trawled through hundreds of websites and elements of marketing materials and noticed a big trend: 80 percent of venues are using the same language. How can anyone stand out and sound different to the Planner if the same language is being used to describe hotels and venues? It makes a commodity of your venue and brings the conversation down to rate.

Planners say that the only reason a decision comes down to rate is if they do not see the difference between how they will achieve better results at one hotel or venue over the next.

If the sales team have not done a good enough job distinguishing their venue then yes, the Planner is left with no choice. They will go for the cheaper option.

I find the language of results is a lot more effective and convincing when trying to convey to a Planner that your venue is the right one. Brochure wording is critical in communicating the atmosphere and priorities of a venue. Features and benefits must be described. However, to stand out, you must take a step further than just describing features and benefits. Too often venues just describe the space, put in a capacity table and don't explain how the venue itself can help the Planner achieve their objectives for organizing the event. This is a critical mistake that many venues make in their pitch and in the positioning of their venue in the marketplace.

Build Your Sales and Marketing Toolkit to Distinguish Your Venue

"Even at the last minute you came up with practical and easy suggestions to help convert the business. Guess what – they worked!"

Bernadette Coffey, Sligo Park Hotel, Ireland.

Powerful Proof - Testimonials

How to have Powerful Proof for the Planner

A testimonial saying, "Oh yes, we had a great conference. Everything went according to plan, the food was delicious, and we got great feedback." just isn't strong enough in today's market. Social Proof is an essential part of your Sales Toolkit. Social Media has taught us to look for more authentic ways to confirm our buying decision. The proof must be from other sources as your word just isn't enough proof anymore. In this section, I will show you how to secure powerful proof for the Planner that yours is the right venue for their event.

However, to get powerful social proof in the form of testimonials, you have to ask for it in a certain way. You have to peel back the layers and get the Planner to tell you what business results they got from having their event at your venue, if they had a higher attendance, or if they got higher satisfaction scores from attendees. That is so much stronger than the Planner just saying we had a great event. It is compelling proof that you can help them achieve the kind of results they want to achieve.

You need a lot of evidence with this market. Just saying it is not strong enough anymore. The Planner just doesn't believe you. You want powerful testimonials to make your marketing materials and your pitch so much more believable and authentic. The strength and effectiveness of a testimonial will all depend on the type of questions you ask your clients when requesting a testimonial.

Having powerful testimonials from your clients is an essential element of your pitch, your lead generating website, brochures and marketing materials. It is also perfect content for social media and around which you can write blog articles. Powerful testimonials work as they are proof that you can do what you say you can do. Planners believe other Planners more than they will believe your word. Testimonials are an important part of your Sales Toolkit that helps you attract the right leads and convert them. We will do more work on developing your Sales Toolkit in a separate section.

Quick tip: When presenting testimonials, they have more weight and credibility when you include a photo of the client with them. All of this is, of course, with client permission. An anonymous testimonial will be better than none; you can make it more effective by including the title of the client and industry sector.

Types of Testimonials

- **Written:** On company letterhead, by email or perhaps a handwritten note.

- **Video:** ensure you have a video testimonial from the different type of clients you want – corporate, Agent, association, team-build, events, etc. Also, it is very powerful to have a video testimonial from a delegate. Planners will want their delegates saying great things about their event, so they are an important source of definitive proof.

- **Verbal:** ask a happy client if you can use them as a reference. Give their name and number to a prospective client so they could call them independently. Obviously, this needs to be a client you have a strong relationship with that is only delighted to do this. If you do not have a client like this, make it your mission to create one. Turn your next event into a client who is your biggest fan.

- **Social media** comments and reviews.

Methodology to Asking for Testimonials

Great testimonials rarely happen of their own accord. It is not often that a client will write a testimonial of the quality that I am speaking about. You have to ask them for it and make it easy for the client to give you that kind of testimonial. Sometimes they need a little prompting on how to do this. I will share with you the wording for that in the next section. First, however, you need to decide whom you are going to ask and how.

A Personal Approach

I love to take the opportunity of asking for testimonials in person or on the phone. It is an opportunity to open up the conversation and ask how you can partner with the client, how else you can be of value to them and what other services would help them to book more business with you? This is all part of the strategic management of an account (which would take another book to go into detail on). Asking for a testimonial as I recommend should be part of the follow-up actions taken with each client after an event. It should be part of your post-event system.

Reviews

Creating tools for receiving more personal reviews.

Rupesh Patel of SmartGuests.com suggests a very easy way to help you get more reviews about your people. After all, that is what reviews should be about — your people and not how clean the hotel was or how great the service was, that is standard. If you want to get more personal reviews to use for your marketing material, Rupesh suggests creating tools to help that happen. A simple tool is to create a personal business card for each staff member. This is for the team to give to guests or Planners whom they know they made a difference to and simply asking them to write a review about their experience. Doing this effectively takes putting in place three small details:

Ensuring each staff member has a business card with their name and role on one side (with contact information) and a Call to

Action on the back – the social review website you would like it on or email address to which they can send their review. For an example of these go to: www.smartguests.com/staff-social-business-cards

Training the team on how to ask for a review or quick testimonial.

Make it very easy for the guest to leave a review/ testimonial while they are still on the property.

It is about making it easy for people to give you a testimonial or review. Most people are delighted to do this; they might forget someone's name or simply just forget to do it even though they had the best of intentions of doing it. When they come across the business card with instructions on how to give the review, it is much easier for them then to get it done.

Powerful Proof

A technical approach to gathering powerful proof.

You can also decide to get very analytical with your approach and open it up to your wider database. You would, therefore, need to employ technology to analyze the responses. Technology such as Survey Monkey, QuestionPro and even forms by Google will all help you to gather and collate your responses. They will only be as powerful as the questions you ask.

Discovering the reason why people have worked with you in the last number of years is always a worthwhile exercise. You might be surprised by some of the answers. What is important however is to understand how your clients want to work with you in the next two to three years.

The most important aspect of all of this is to use the client's exact wording. Don't paraphrase it or put it into your marketing or industry lingo. Your client's words are what will help you to attract more of the same kind of client.

Achieving The WIN with This Technique

How Bernadette won a piece of business worth a considerable amount to her hotel using this technique.

Bernadette used a testimonial to close a piece of business that was worth a considerable amount to the hotel in the challenging month of November. What was key in her use of the testimonial is two-fold:

1. The type of testimonial she used (she matched it to the client).
2. The timing.

To give you a little background on this, I called Bernadette one day to check how my online program she had just signed up for was going for her. She had just started it and hadn't yet applied all of the techniques to help her convert more business. I asked her was there anything she was working on right now, that she was trying to close that perhaps I could help her with.

She told me of a great piece of business that she was very anxious to convert. She was waiting to hear from the client the next days as to whether she had won it or not. The committee was meeting that night to make their final decision on the venue. Bernadette shared that there were three regions bidding for the business. She was competing with one other hotel in her region plus the hotels in the other regions.

Bernadette had uncovered the lead herself, got placed on the RFP list and had done well by getting the committee to her hotel for lunch. She had met most of the client's parameters to be in the running as the chosen venue. She felt she had done everything she could at this step. Even at this late stage, I knew there was more she could do on the all-important decision-making day.

I discussed with Bernadette that her contact was very anxious to win the business for her region (Sligo). It was important to her reputation and her visibility within the organization and in her job role that she secures the event for the region. This was the angle to take with the client rather than trying to win the business for Bernadette's hotel. Bernadette had to take on the role of partnering with her client to win it for Sligo, to boost the client's reputation.

I gave her four options she could do at this late hour. She chose to take action on this one.

Call the client. Ask what she could do to help her win the business for Sligo (Sligo being the city). What is also important about asking this question is to have a few suggestions in case the client says "I don't know" or "there is nothing you can do at this step."

After our conversation, Bernadette sat back for a minute. She told me she thought about the business *even more* from the client's perspective and not from hers. She did call her client, and she asked her:

"What can I do today to help you win the business for Sligo?"

This immediately positioned Bernadette as a partner, instead of a supplier as she was showing that she was trying to win the business together.

They decided that having a testimonial to read out at the meeting would help. Bernadette chose a testimonial from a similar client, one that she knew they would identify with. This was important. Always try to match the testimonial with the client or the industry/ type of business or the outcomes. They will want to read about another organization that achieved similar outcomes from holding their event with you.

Guess what? She won it! The client called Bernadette at 10.15pm that night to let her know the great news. Now, Bernadette had obviously done many things right up to that point to help her win the business. She is also a wonderful person to work with, and she truly cares about the client's event. However, she does believe that the last minute phone call and testimonial helped her to win the business.

Client Testimonials

Questions to Help Your Clients Share Powerful Testimonials

When working with Jeanine Blackwell, she sent me wording on how to ask for a testimonial. I have found it effective and have used it a few times myself to help me get the kind of testimonials I needed. I have adapted the wording to suit the conference market, and I am sharing that with you below.

Greetings/Hello <insert name>,

*We are doing some research to help us evaluate the specific value that we create in partnership with our clients. As part of this process, I am asking some of my favorite clients for feedback, and you are one. I would appreciate your feedback about the areas of **strength and results** that have been created through our working together and indeed you holding your events at this property/venue.*
Please share what you consider being my strengths in working with you or that of the team and the venue along with specific examples of when these strengths created value for you.

You could begin your response with:

"One of the greatest ways that you add value is..."
or
"The biggest result we got from working with you is..."

Notice that in the example above you are giving the client an opportunity to share how you were of value to them. You can decide yourself what clients you know well enough to send this to, or you can just leave it as asking about the value the venue or the team brought to them.

If you would like to download this wording to use to gather your testimonials, go to:

www.ConferenceConverter.com/bookresources

If you would like to send your clients a quick survey to help you uncover the above information and get a little more specific with them regarding what their challenges are in running an event, I have created a one-page survey for you. It is available in my online program "How to Build Your Sales Toolkit." It is a great way to connect with clients and engage with the people with whom you have done business.

In the online program I share lots of extra resources on how to build authentic, believable material that almost does the selling for you.

Action Items from This Section:

- Write your top 5 clients names here:
  1. _____
  2. _____
  3. _____
  4. _____
  5. _____

- Ask these top 5 clients – what results do you help them achieve by working with you?

Floor Plans

The Secret Weapon of the Conference Industry and How to Make Them Brilliant

"Floor Plans when well designed are the secret weapon in the conference and event industry."

Ciara Feely,
Creator of the Conference Converter System™; Author.

The floor plan is an essential tool to have in any Sales Toolkit. It is a valuable document that will communicate immediately to the organizer that you understand their needs and think like them if it is done correctly.

Floor plans should be as detailed as possible and immediately from one glance orientate the Planner.

They should help your future clients to figure out exactly where the main meeting space is with reference to the rest of the hotel or venue. Conference Planners want to know where each door out of the conference room leads to so they can control where their delegates can go to, one Planner even used the words "escape to." A well-executed floor plan document can give you *the edge over your competitor*.

After ten years of searching for venues online, I have experienced thousands of floor plans. Most I have come across leave the Planner feeling a little frustrated with too many questions still unanswered. They are outlines of the room itself. They do not orientate the Planner or give them a sense of where the meeting room is in regard to the rest of the hotel or venue. Ideally, the Planner should be able to picture exactly where their delegates will be throughout the day from one glance at the floor plans. If they can do this from your website and floor plans, they will want to call your venue, eager to talk business.

Put yourself in the shoes of a Planner for a minute and think what are the questions they have that floor plans need to answer? Questions such as:

- How long does it take to get 200 people from the car park to the conference room and how is that managed?

- Where can attendees escape to once you do get them in the conference room?
- What's the view from the room? What can delegates see?
- How far is the catering, exhibition or breakout area from the main conference room?

Badly designed Floor Plans result in lost business.

I was working with a UK professional conference organizing company. They were not able to come to Ireland for a site inspection and so relied on me as a Venue Finder to be their eyes, and advise them accordingly. To be able to choose the right venue remotely like this, they also needed the hotel to have detailed information for them to establish if their exhibition and conference would fit comfortably.

However, the floor plans the hotel had were not detailed. The hotel assumed the Planner would be able to come for a site tour, and they did not have any detail on the floor plans. This is a dangerous assumption to make as fewer site inspections are happening. You also really have to prove to the Planner before they will even consider a site tour that you are worth an investment of their time.

Planners have little time to spend checking out lots of venues. You have to get on the very short list of venues being considered before you win the opportunity for a site tour.

I sent the floor plans I received from the hotel to the Planner, named Mark. Mark called me straight away and asked: "Ciara, does this hotel run many conferences with exhibition space requirements? Based on these floor plans I don't think they do.

I couldn't possibly make a decision based on this information." He could not believe they didn't have more detail in their floor plans. What's worse, it made him doubt their suitability for the event. Both the venue and I, as an Agent, had lost credibility because of the floor plans. He was no longer confident that they could handle his event.

This is what I did to restore his confidence:
I had to take the hotel floor plans and draw my own set (luckily I knew the layout of the hotel well). I then had to write in the details that were missing. I had to go back to the hotel three times asking for measurements of the networking area, the width of the doors, the measurements of their buffet tables and the size of each room when the divider walls were up.

I also wrote in details such as where the lobby was, where the entrance door was, where the car park was, where the restaurant and bar was, what each door in the conference room opened out onto, where the stage would be set up and what the windows looked out onto. Finally, I had to draw where the breakout rooms were in relation to the plenary room.

I had to reassure him that the venue was right for his event and walk him through the floor plans that I made up. I had to trust he would take my word for it. He did. The hotel turned out to be perfect for his event, and he went on to book it annually, but his first impression was that it would not suit because of the floor plans.

Must-Have "Checklist" for Brilliant Floor Plans

I've created a checklist on what to include in floor plans that will help the Planner to say **YES**. This checklist will show you how to create a valuable sales tool for your property. It has a lot of detail in it. Some will apply to all venues; some of it is for larger event venues. You have to be clever with the way you present all of this information; however, having it at hand is critical to converting business. You only have to gather this information once, and then you have it for years.

 It will save hours of time trying to gather it at different times for different quotes. I share it with participants in my online workshop on how to create your **Conference Converter Toolkit™**. I also review your floor plans and give feedback on how to make them super "Planner Friendly."

If you create floor plans as I have outlined, I guarantee they will help you to **WIN** more business as it immediately says to the Event Planner that you get them, that you understand their needs, and you and your team will help them to organize a great event.

Just think how you make the Planner feel when you are making it so easy for them at the beginning steps of their buying process. When you gather all of this information, information that the Planner needs to make a decision, you are immediately communicating to them that you are going to make their life so much easier on the all-important day of their event. It is immediate proof, and it is helping you to build the level of trust and confidence that they need to say **YES** to your venue.

Personalizing the Floor Plan

The easiest way to do this is to print out the floor plans and write in which room you envision will work for each aspect of their event. Having CAD Drawings of your venue that you can personalize by drawing certain set-ups would impress and make life easy for the Planner. Point out everything, color code the plans using different colors perhaps for different aspects of the event or different days.

Another brilliant way to help the Planner is to create a video for them. Create a simple video of you walking them through the floor plans, pointing out where each part of their event will take place. I have put together a sample video of how to do this effectively which I share with participants in my online program.

Floor Plan Technology

There is such exciting technology available now that will help you make it easy for the Planner to visualize their event at your venue. There are lots of options out there, so I have put together a quick glance summary highlighting the features and practical application of each.

This is a highlight of just a few of the floor plan technologies that will help you to **WIN** more business:

3D Floor Plans bring your event to life. They are a wonderful tool to use that will help the Planner visualize their event at your venue. Numerous companies are producing them. However, it is important to guide them in what they need to show. Most 3D plans I have seen only show the room itself and don't bring to life the space outside the conference rooms. This is vital space to show the Planner so they can get a sense of how their event will flow and how easy it is to move people from point A to B.

There are very smart programs available that create personalized room plans. Set-ups for individual events can be drawn, tables moved around, enabling the organizer to design their event in your conference space, picture it and therefore feel confident booking the venue. This technology makes it so easy for Event Planners to book with you.

These are some examples; it is worth the investment and some are free.

Social Tables (.com) Helping you create visual planning tools to increase conversion rates. They are simple to use. The functionality includes diagramming that your team or the Planner can use, seating charts that make it so easy to move around tables and finalize the look of the room. They also have check-in software that the Planner can use onsite.
What I love is that this software can be used on your website to increase the number of direct RFPs you receive and your conversion rates. Your capacity charts and rooms can be customized for each Planner making it easy for them to visualize their event at your venue.

Meeting Matrix.com and iPlan The Planner can sign up for a free account and can change the room layout according to their needs. You must place a link on your website to enable this.

Magic Plan (an app) This is an app where the Planner can create their own floor plans as they walk through the venue with you.

Alternatively, you have it done in advance, and they can write notes on the iPad as you do the walk through with them. It is a bit tricky this app; it does take a little getting used to. The big advantage though is that the Planner will have their own personalized floor plans with their notes after the site tour. This will help them to visualize their event at your venue.

Top Table Planner (.com) Planners can arrange the seating of their guests with one click. They can add tables and move around the guests at the last minute; it simplifies the whole process. There is a free version of this also. Letting the Planner know about this type of technology, that will make their life easy, just adds to your credibility and partner status with them. When thinking about the level of detail to go into with floor plans, put yourself in the shoes of a Conference Organizer. Each day they put their reputation on the line booking venues as there is always a fear of getting it wrong. See how easy it is to picture organizing and controlling where 300 people go on your property. **You will then see what a vital part of your job it is to make booking your venue as easy as possible from the desk of the Conference Planner.**

WIN Big Budget Corporate Business

In putting together this section, I consulted not just with Meeting Planners, but with technical production experts too. Maarten Vanneste of Abbit Technology (www.abbit.eu) and The Meeting Institute and Brandt Krueger (www.brandtkrueger. com) gave me this advice for venues that want to go after the big business, the corporate business that spends half a million on production alone. For 75 percent of the bigger projects the production company is asked to recommend suitable venues. If you are making it easy for production companies to work with you, then it will help to get you on the list of venues being considered. If this type of information is easily found on your website, ready to download, then you are definitely on the list. This is the type of detail that becomes important in those bigger budget events.

The most important detail is to have a full photo of the room with this information – not a part of the room or a zoom in on certain detail. They must be able to see the whole of the room in order to plan the production, AV and equipment correctly.

The detailed room plan and floor plan go hand in hand with this. Work with your operations and tech team to get as much detail as possible to produce your own "Production Crew Fact Sheet." I have an outline of one put together. It's another one of the valuable resources I share with my online **Conference Converter Toolkit™** program participants.

If not addressed up front, the details a production crew need can all add unplanned expenses to setting up an event and can cause problems if it is not thought about beforehand. You cannot always rely on the Planner having thought of it. If you take the lead on this, you are positioning yourself as a valuable resource to the Planner in saving them last minute headaches and costs. The production experts I spoke with have seen problems arise at many older style hotels and venues, where equipment has had to be brought in through the kitchen and up and down different levels before making it to the ballroom. Whether or not you have a venue that has easy loading areas, you have to talk about it up front. It is your role to help the Planner to foresee problems that may arise at other venues.

They will appreciate the advice.

As Maarten says: "Nobody thinks of the details of AV and production. Most people mainly focus on the food and drink." Supporting the production experts may help you to win the business as these experts already work with a lot of the type of Planners with whom you want to do business. A recommendation from experts like this who have already earned the Planners trust and confidence is golden.

Space by Numbers

Capacity Charts

This is a small but important point that drives Planners mad. What Planners find very frustrating is to discover that the numbers just don't add up. If what the capacity chart states will fit and what they believe will fit in terms of numbers just don't match, then you have lost credibility. You are better off having the conversation with the Planner that the room fits 300 people, but ideally, 270 are comfortable. You will be respected for saying that and earn a lot more trust.

I regularly notice that the maximum capacity numbers on a website might vary to those in the brochure and might even vary in different pages on the website. This sends alarm bells off in the head of the Planner if they see different numbers in your marketing materials.

Double check your capacity chart to ensure it is in line with the following guidelines that Planners use.

Theatre Style

Less than 60 people = 12 sq. ft./1.12m² per person

60-300 people = 11 sq. ft./1.02m² per person

300+ people = 10 sq. ft./0.93m² per person

Classroom Style

Less than 60 people = 22 sq. ft./2.04m² per person

60-300 people = 20 sq. ft./1.86m² per person

300+ people = 17 sq. ft./1.58m² per person

Banquet Style

1-300+ people = 13.5 sq. ft./1.25m² per person

Conference Style

300+ people = 30 sq. ft./2.79m² per person

Hollow Square or Rectangle

1-45+ people = 30 sq. ft./2.79m² per person

(Not recommended for over 45 people)

U-Shape

1-60+ people = 35 sq./3.25m² per person

(Not recommended for over 45 people)

Source: MPI resources.

Action Items from This Section:

Put yourself in the shoes of the Planner. See how easy it is for them to visualize an event from your floor plans. How easy is it for them to see how can they move 300 delegates from A to B and how quickly can they do it by only using your floor plans?

Download the following:

- How to use Google Maps Floor Plans.

- A video on how to create brilliant floor plans.

Free Downloads Here:

www.ConferenceConverter.com/bookresources

Building Your Sales Toolkit

Your Website – How to Turn It into A Lead Generation Machine

"Ciara's program showed me how to get the Planner calling the hotel with their fingers crossed hoping that we have their dates available."

Michelle, Director of Sales of an Independent Property.

Is your website **a lead generation machine?** **60 percent of the decision to buy or not can be made online (according to a Harvard Business Review).** Do your prospects call you, excited they found you? As a Venue Finder, when I found a website that I loved, one that gave me the information I was looking for, I called the venue with my fingers crossed hoping that they had my dates available. Those are the leads that are so much easier to convert.

You can double your conversion rate by generating more direct leads via your website. The module on building an effective web page shows you how to do this.

According to MPI data, there is an 87 percent decrease in the RFP closing ratio from just 7 years ago. What that means for you and your team is that hours of sales time is wasted before winning a lead.

That is down to three reasons:

1. There are **less staff in a sales office** compared to a number of years ago.

2. **RFP Spam** – RFP technology has exploded the number of RFPs being sent out to hotels or venues. You know yourself, the same lead can be sent to fifty hotels with the touch of a button. The chapter on "How to Write Proposals that **WIN**" will help with this problem.

3. Venues are **making it hard to buy**! Clients are not getting enough information up front on the website to help them make a decision. So they have to send out their specifications to numerous properties to help them filter out venues that are not suitable.

The First Step of the Decision-Making Process

The Planner makes a decision on what venue to book based on a number of steps that they go through. So you must help them by making it easy for them to say **YES** at each step. Right at the very beginning of the project to find a suitable venue, they are not necessarily ready to speak to the sales person. They want to do independent research first; most of this research is done online.

Based on the experience they have had online, they then come up with their list of venues to contact. Again, they may not be ready to speak to every venue yet, they might add in another step in their filter such as the proposal (I cover how to write proposals that win in another chapter). The website or the description used in the 3rd party Agent's website is a massive influencer to help you get through to the next stage of the decision-making process. So it has to be right. You simply must get past this all-important step in order to get the opportunity to bid for this business.

I posted this question in the Event Management LinkedIn group **"What do venues do that drives you mad?"** I got over 109 comments with constructive feedback within 72 hours. 90 percent of the comments were all about communication. So the great news is they can all be fixed. I'll go into detail about that in subsequent chapters.

The second biggest bugbear for them was not getting the kind of information they needed when they needed it. The website being a big source of frustration. I share with you what comments were made about the website in my online program on how to build a powerful Sales Toolkit.

www.ConferenceConverter.com/connect

A venues website is the main tool that they use to help them start to trust the venue and figure out if it is a fit for their event. Yet, it is the main source of annoyance for most Planners and leaves them feeling utterly frustrated. That is not the emotion you want to be evoking at this early stage of their buying process.

Let me ask you this:

- Do you think **your venue is the same as the next**?

- Do you think decisions should come down to rate?

Planners tell me the only time a decision comes down to rate is when they don't see the difference between venues. When the team haven't distinguished how their hotel will help them achieve better results from their conference by holding it at one venue over the next.

Your power sales tools such as the website are what will **distinguish your venue – why**; because that is what the Planner uses to make their decisions.

The average attention span online is about eight seconds. 1,2,3,4,5,6,7,8.

It's critical that your home page and conference page **Attract** the Planner to want to engage with you. It makes conversion so much easier. Otherwise they are gone and the lead opportunity is lost forever.

What is your Website saying to a Meeting Planner about your venue?

A lot!

The power of a venue's website is massive and it is a very powerful tool to use to engage with the Meeting Planner. It is either saying: "We do conferences, very often and very well. Here is all the information you need to feel comfortable booking a conference, exhibition or event with us." Or it is saying: "We don't have a lot of photography or detailed floor plans on the conference space. We really don't understand your needs by not having these available but we would, of course, love your conference business. We will first make it hard for you to picture or imagine your conference here; we will then make you come visit us to prove to you that we can do it!"

A properly constructed website or conference web page can help you to build immediate trust and confidence with your prospective clients. Those are the kind of emotions you want to stir in prospective clients. The right web page can catapult you through the first few steps of building a relationship with the client because they will immediately see that you get them and their world. It can really help to position you as a partner instead of being a supplier. That is the kind of website I can help you to build.

Which scenario would you prefer?

One where a Planner absolutely loves your website, you have made it easy for them so far and so demonstrating that you will be easy to work with (and save them time). They are excited that they found you and really want to call you to progress with the sale. Would you prefer to be working with a warm sales prospect like this who is considering you as their partner?

Or what a badly constructed web page can do is really annoy Planners. This results in two scenarios:

1. They will *not* call you – and call your competitor instead.

2. They call you but they are now looking at you as just their supplier. Or perhaps they just want to get a quote from you because they need to get three quotes. They have no intention of booking with you, so you are never going to convert the lead. This is the worst scenario as it wastes such valuable sales time.

Which relationship would you prefer? What relationship is going to help you skip through about three steps of their sales process? Which type of relationship will convert the lead quicker?

If your website isn't properly set up to engage with the Planner in the way they want to be engaged with then it means you have to do all the hard work. It's like pushing them along. It's like a cold call which is a slow and sometimes disheartening process. It will force the Planner to negotiate with you based on price. They haven't seen the value you or your venue can bring to the table so they don't see why they should pay more.

The first impression has been made on the website and that has stuck in their mind. The experience you want the Planner to have with you begins on the website and in your marketing resources.

A website designed with the needs of the Planner in mind,

simply pulls in the Planner. It's a magnet for leads. It is much easier to have the website do the pulling for you. There are too many opportunities lost otherwise. In my online workshops I share great examples of websites that work for Planners. The website is an opportunity to develop warmed up leads for your team. Leads that are so much easier to convert.

The Planners experience of you and working with your venue starts on the website. It must excite them, give them confidence and make them want to engage with your sales team. Those kinds of prospects are so much easier to convert and are happy to pay your rates.

In developing my program on "How to Turn your Website into a Lead Generation Machine," I searched websites worldwide. Looking for an experience that excited me as the client. I bring brilliant examples of websites that work together in this module. I walk you through how to create a brief to just hand to your web developer. If you don't have the budget to redo your website now or if you are part of a brand and are limited in what you can do, I have some easy fixes for that too. There are quick tweaks that will deliver more hot leads for your sales team.

Action Items from This Section:

If you would like to have the result of doubling your conversion rate on leads generated directly from your website, let's talk. If you would like to turn website traffic into conference sales, feel free to contact us for an in-depth website review on how conference friendly your website is.

We will create an easy-to-implement report packed with simple action items which will have a dramatic effect on your website conversion rates. This can be given directly to your website designer to implement.

www.ConferenceConverter.com/connect

Build Your Marketing Toolkit

More Meaningful Marketing

"We all think we know how to sell hotels, Ciara just turns it all on its head. Absolutely inspirational!"
Lisa Stewart, Best Western Hotels International.

I just love the tagline from Change Agents an Irish marketing firm – More Meaningful Marketing. Their ethos is about connecting with people instead of trying to sell to them. That is the key to attracting more of your ideal clients, clients that are easier to convert. It will have a dramatic effect on your conversion rate.

Your marketing resources are an important tool the Planner uses to help them make a decision. It is important to get a **YES** at this step in their buying process. They are looking for consistencies in your approach to this market. Your conversation, pitch, website and marketing resources must all be in sync and consistent in the message being communicated. I hesitate to use the phrase "sales brochure;" as in today's market, the sales brochure must not be "salesy."

That is why I prefer to refer to your sales brochures as marketing resources and that is what I'll show you how to build. They are created for the client to help them to buy. Yes, they must be informative and relay the important information about your venue. However, the information must be presented in such a way that it is all about the client and helping them to find the right venue. They must feel that it was created to help them, not sell to them.

It is really important to know where you stand with your target clients. I am going to tell you how a Planner is reading your sales brochure and floor plans now. I will give you some examples and you will know yourself if that is the message you are communicating now and indeed if it is the message you mean to communicate. This will help you to know if you need to change it or not, because what you are saying, what the website is communicating, what the "sales brochure" is messaging to your clients, that is all affecting your ability to convert conferences and events.

In this section I will talk about how to attract the right leads in the first place because they are ten times easier to convert than a lead that isn't the right fit. Having the right sales collateral in place will help you to attract more leads and importantly more of the right leads. We speak about this further in another chapter when we profile the **Perfect Fit Planner™**.

Why change? Planners no longer believe traditional "Sales Brochures."

The challenges of the Conference Planner have changed dramatically in the last two years and you need to be addressing these in your marketing and sales approach. Their needs, their problems, their worries, their client's needs, the needs of the delegates have changed. So what you are saying in your marketing resources and sales collateral must reflect these changes. When you hold the Planners interest, sound different to them and stand out, that will in turn influence the Planner to book with you.

When is the last time you sat down and completely rewrote the material you use every day to help you do your job? When your client's needs change, your message to attract them must too. If you haven't changed the conversation you have with the Planner, your pitch and the ultimate message you are communicating in these materials, it is time to make a change. That is what we are going to touch on in this chapter. What the Planner needs to see in your sales material in order to say **YES**. This will help you to get to the next step in the clients buying process.

When sales materials are crafted correctly, they take the focus away from rate. I know over the last number of years it seems like decisions are only being made based on rate. I can tell you they are not if you are distinguishing your property effectively.

But you must be hitting all of their hot buttons and giving them everything they need in your sales tools and in your whole approach to this market in order to take the focus off rate. You simply have to switch the focus to what they are really buying. Your pitch from their very first interaction with you must be selling past the price. The marketing resources you create will help you to do that.

It is all about creating believable, authentic material; material that is not salesy or pushy. We need to create a resource that is helpful to the client and answers the Planners questions, while, building **trust and confidence** that you and your team really understand their needs, can help them and will help them to run an amazing event.

I mentioned Shawna Suckow, the head of SPIN — a group of senior Planners. When interviewing her for this section she told me Planners just don't believe traditional sales and marketing messages any more. So who do they believe? They believe their peers and other Meeting Planners, they believe their delegates and they believe what complete strangers are saying on social media. So your sales material must change to reflect this new authentic messaging.

Having the right sales collateral in place will help you to attract more leads. Creating marketing material that is specific for your property and your ideal client will help you to attract the right kind of leads and convert them more quickly.

I am not going to outline your social media and digital strategy in this book. That would be a book in itself and I have a lot of it detailed in my online program. It is a lot easier to show you in video and photography how to do that in my training website. I will show you how to be more effective with the money you are spending on marketing for the meetings market.

I go into detail on how to create your sales and marketing resources with my online program participants. I also review your material. If you would like this client's perspective or help in crafting your materials for this market, connect with me at:

www.ConferenceConverter.com/connect

Powerful Print

By Andy Rogers of Xpedient Print, www.XpedientPrint.co.uk; Contributing Author.

"In the digital world, there is a lot of noise. The right printed material can have a huge impact. Print helps you to cut through this noise. It is tactile; it has gravitas and shows how serious and credible your business is. When done right – it helps you to Stand Out!"

Andy Rogers, Xpedient Print.

Getting the Look and Feel of the Print Material Right

I have had many conversations with Andy about print. I've been sent so many "brochures" and received so many at different tradeshows. Getting the look and feel of it right is just as powerful as the message you write on it. So I asked him to share a few of the tips he has seen work over his lifetime of working with print.

5 Tips to Make Print More Powerful

Tip 1. Know What You Want to Achieve
When deciding on what print you are going to use you first have to decide how it will fit into your overall marketing campaign. Print is much more powerful when used as part of a strategy and not just in isolation. Better results are delivered when print is used alongside email campaigns or print alongside an in-person contact such as at a tradeshow.

What is it you want to achieve from your brochure, postcard or newsletter?

- Maybe you want your print to raise awareness.
- It could be to drive traffic to your website or special offer.
- You may want to encourage more phone enquires or generate site tours of your property.

Whatever you want it to do, don't try to do everything at once. Where possible it will be much more effective if it has a single purpose with a single message you want to convey. This will make the process easier for you and will have a bigger impact and ultimately return on investment.

Tip 2. Know Your Target Market
Decide who is the target market, sector, companies, position within company and even names if possible. The more specific you are the more appealing you can make your messaging and presentation. If people feel the message, tone, offering and value is directed specifically at their needs then it will get the desired reaction.

You may need more than one piece of print for each of your

markets. For example, a financial company would use different language than a medical company or a high-tech company so if you want to appeal to them, ideally speak their language in your marketing message.

This will increase the price but if you are more targeted you will convert more.

If you are not sure about your messaging and understanding what the end user actually wants, then I suggest you speak to your existing clients. Do some easy market research; ask them why they use you? Which elements of what you do or offer appeal to them. You may be surprised by their responses and it may not be what you thought.

Tip 3. Budgets
Most of the time print decisions are driven by cost. Usually as it's at the end of the process it's about shaving costs. This is always a mistake.

I am not saying that it shouldn't be cost effective for what you want to achieve but stripping back on paper quality and finish won't deliver what it was intended to in the first place. You will be disappointed with the results; all of these tips are to help you get a much bigger return on investment.

Your print is often a representation of your business, company, product or offering. Do you want that first impression to be cheap or inexpensive?

Your print will always make an impression on someone so make sure it's a good one.

I see print as an investment and not a cost. Think of the cost of losing out on that next conference booking by not making the right impression.

Quality can be cost effective, it can:

- Enhance your credibility
- Build a quality relationship with potential clients
- Build confidence
- Deliver impact
- Achieve much bigger results and **WIN** more business

That's when print can be powerful.

Tip 4. Preparation

There are a few areas to consider when preparing to create effective print resources:

a. **Great copy** that delivers the message well and understanding the way the end user would like it, is really important. Less is more, most of the time. Don't be tempted to fill pages with technical information. Most print is about generating a strong feeling or emotional bond before you sell. People need to feel connected and they buy from the heart. Your printed material needs to demonstrate that you understand their concerns, worries or needs and have experience in dealing with those effectively. I would suggest you use a copywriter here. This element is often under-valued; however, making your message clear will have a more powerful impact.

b. **Photography** is key to the style and look of your printed material. You have heard the saying "a picture is worth a 1000 words" and it can be crucial on the impact of your material. Again first impression counts and pictures connect on an emotional level. Avoid stock photos. If you use a photographer to get great, authentic images you can deliver your message more quickly.

c.   **Design**. With your designer and printer, you can choose the size and layout of the brochure or materials. Great design is worth its weight in gold. It's not about putting pretty pictures on a page. If you are investing in material that you want to deliver serious results, then the look and feel is key.

Fonts, color palettes, branding, it all plays an important part and when pulled together creates a visually impactful result that positively reinforces your objectives. The size of the printed material should also suit the style of the photos – for example landscape pictures are more suited to a larger size document such as A4 landscape.

Tip 5. The Print Itself

I have produced various videos covering specific elements such as paper choice, sizes, number of pages and additional finishes. There are lots of things to consider but knowing how you want people to feel when they receive your printed material will guide you when choosing. I suggest you take a look at the videos in Ciara's online program to get a fuller understanding of the importance of these elements on impact. These videos are part of the marketing module Ciara has created. Details are at the end of this chapter on how to access this program.

When print is used best as a part of a wider plan, the follow-up is key. So where possible make sure you have a mechanism to enable a follow-up call to action. This could take the format of:

✓ a specific number for them to call

✓ a promo code

✓ directing them to a specific landing page

✓ QR codes are very effective for bringing your target message directly to where you want them

Having a clear call to action on your printed material means you can measure the return on investment of your print jobs. In my online workshop on **How to Craft Marketing Resources that practically do the Selling for You**, I go into detail that will help you to get a quicker return on investment from your print marketing. Along with a full review of your marketing resources, I help you to tell the story of your venue in a way that is compelling to the Meeting Planner. Andy Rogers also shares the insider tips on the print industry and how to save time, hassle and money in working with your printer. We cover more of the important print details to get right such as;

1. The materials to use to make the first impression you want to make.

2. The design.

3. Paper size, Paper quality.

4. Font options, The use of Colors.

5. Different effects for different results.

6. How to avoid unnecessary delays and costs in dealing with a printer!

Action Items from This Section:

- Ask a good client to critically analyze your own marketing material. Ask them to imagine that they did not know your property. Would your marketing material be effective for them in that scenario?

If you want a great partner to help you achieve the results you want to achieve from your print marketing resources, connect with Andy andy@xpedientprint.co.uk. www.XpedientPrint.co.uk.

The Power Of Photography To WIN More Group Business

Powerful Photography

Powerful photography is powerful proof to the Planner that your property is the right fit for their event. It is also an effective tool to help you get to YES more quickly.

The photography on the home page of a hotel website must engage the Planner straight away and whisper to them **"We do Congresses and Events."** If your website photography leans too much to the leisure and weddings market, it is an immediate turn off for Conference and Meeting Planners. I'm not suggesting not to appeal to the leisure and weddings market on the home page – people will naturally gravitate towards what they are looking for – an interesting photo of the main conference room and a separate conference/meetings tab will suffice in getting them to click through.

A lack of photography and video is saying to a Meeting Planner and Conference Planner "We just don't want your business *enough.*" I can't tell you how many times I hear sales people tell me they don't have a picture of a room set up in a certain style or of the networking space.

I have seen a lot of photography on websites and in marketing brochures that are a turn off for the Planner. Here are a few.

Photography No-Nos! Ways to help you lose business!

- Photos of a wedding on the conference page or brochure.

- Photos of the board room table with close up on the note pad, pen and bottled water.

- Photo of a laptop and two people sitting around it smiling.

- Stock photography – you have no chance of distinguishing your property if a few venues are using the same photos.

- Photo of half of the room and nothing else, show its full size.

- Just showing empty rooms. Planners want to see what the room looks like with people in it.

- Photos not being representative of the room or playing a trick on the eye. For example: The King size bed replaced by a double bed to make the room look bigger, I have seen this done.

Planners need proof of how it will feel to work with you and your team and a photo will go a long way to helping them form that emotional attachment to your property. I have lots of ideas put together in the Marketing Toolkit to show you how to build a strong emotional attachment with potential clients using photography and free technology tools. In my Agent days I remember having to hop into the car so many times to take my own photos and videos to prove to a Planner why I thought a particular property was at least worth a site inspection! I've put this module together so I never have to do that again.

The Use of Video to Help You Convert and Attract Leads

Video makes it **easy** for a client to visualize their event at your hotel or venue.

Syndacast predicts that 74 percent of all internet traffic in 2017 will be video. And James McQuivey, Ph.D. of Forrester research has told us that a *one-minute video is worth 1.8 million words*.

Meeting and Conference Planners have less and less time these days, they are double jobbing. The days of being able to do a site inspection at six properties is gone. Virtual site tours will become standard for smaller events. Some Planners don't even do a site tour for events under a certain value as the budget or time just isn't available.

Having a 360° tour or video of your meeting rooms is imperative in attracting, converting and winning meetings and conference business in the next few years.

It immediately says, "We know you need to be sure that this is a suitable venue for your conference. Before you take your valuable time out of the office to see it in person, here is a video we put together of the space so you can be assured you are not wasting your time by coming for a site tour." It says **"We get you! We are on your wave length,"** "**We understand your needs – it is great to work with us.**" "**We will make your life easy!**" I've said it before in this book, but it is worth repeating. If you are making life easy for the Planner at this stage of their buying process, then you are going to make their life easy on delivery of the event.

*51.9% of marketing professionals worldwide name video as the type of content with the best ROI.

(*Source Digital Marketing Blog)

Most hotel videos at the moment have two photos of the conference room at the very end of a four-minute-plus video, making the Conference Organizer have to wait till the end to see what they want to see. This is very frustrating. Create a short video of the meeting space and put it on your website and social media channels.

Tip from an Expert: Vincent Walshe of IntenetSuccess.ie advised to name each scene on the video – main conference room, networking area, lobby, standard guestroom etc. Remember that those who are watching it do not know your property at all and like to know what they are looking at.

Build Your Tech Toolkit

- **Technology Trends**
- **Apps**
- **Augmented and Virtual Reality**
- **Projection Mapping**
- **Virtual Site Inspections**
- **Wi-Fi**

How to Get into the Pocket of Every Conference and Meeting Delegate

I asked Corbin to contribute to this chapter as he is recognized as one of the Top 25 Most Influential People in the meetings industry and has been for years. He is top of his game when it comes to Conference Technology and the recognized "Go to Expert" in this area worldwide.

For my part, mobile technology has fundamentally changed the meetings and conference industry over the last number of years and will make the biggest impact on it for the next five! It is an opportunity for Conference Planners and Hotels/Venues to be in the pocket of every conference delegate – what an opportunity! Corbin's chapter has lots of insights and predictions on how to get there.

"Meetings are going to change more in the next five years than they did in the last five years due to Social Media and Mobile Technology," according to Corbin.

One trend is for sure, the key service for a hotel or venue to provide is excellent Wi-Fi access – that is free!

These are exciting times. The rate of technology change is accelerating with thousands of ideas, apps and innovations bubbling up to help venues, Meeting Planners, exhibitors and other meeting participants to do their jobs better. Corbin is currently tracking over 300 Meeting Planner technology companies; there is an explosion happening in the market, and it is essential to embrace and understand the power of event technology.

What is important for hotels and venues is that they are up to date, using and helping their clients to get the most from technology with their events.

Your knowledge of how technology can enhance your sales process, help you to attract, convert and win more conference business is critical. If you want to be considered a serious candidate in your industry and build your profile like that, read on...

Top Technology Trends

By Corbin Ball; Contributing Author.

1. Crowdsourcing and Crowd Sharing

Crowdsourcing is the process of obtaining services, ideas, answers or content from a large group of people (typically an online community) rather than from traditional suppliers. A big benefit is better input. James Latham of International Meetings Review describes it as "The Wisdom of Crowds" or "Collective Intelligence." The important point is it is being driven by audiences and the application of social media. The days of the Conference Planner deciding what the content of a conference will be are limited. The trend is towards letting the delegates decide what they want to discuss and indeed for letting them answer questions and share their knowledge during the sessions.

This is altering the fundamentals of meeting design and architecture. Pooling the intellect of the room and letting the audience set the agenda is a big conference trend. Speakers have to become accomplished facilitators to control the flow of information and keep the conference on track. This means that excellent Wi-Fi is even more critical at conferences and events.

It must be strong enough to ensure a few hundred or thousand can be online at the same time.

A range of crowdsourcing tools has emerged for sharing, funding, voting and much more. Benefits include lower costs and greater choice, all of which can be used in a variety of ways for events. This will change the way meeting participants find and book sleeping rooms (hoteliers watch out!) with airbnb.com and easynest.com; share travel with sunyride.com, airbaltic. satisly.com; co-create event content with panelpicker.sxsw.com, allourideas.org, ideascale.com, stereopill.com, review events with yelp.com, hubb.it, event-rate.com and fund/promote events with peoplefund.it, planana.com, picatic.com, tixelated. com, to name a few. Additionally, mobile audience polling devices have been in use for a while now during an event for insight capture, market research and real-time feedback to assist in making strategic decision-making.

2. Virtual Reality and Augmented Reality (VR and AR)

I will walk you through a full explanation of these technologies and practical applications of them as they apply to the world of venue sales in the next section of this chapter.

Both of these technologies have huge implications for group collaboration, virtual training, interactive design and site tours.

Microsoft's HoloLens is an advanced AR system with gesture controls. It involves see-through holographic computer enabling high-definition holograms to come to life in your world, integrating with your physical places, spaces and things. Holograms mixed with your real world will unlock all-new ways to create, communicate, work and play. This has huge potential for group collaboration, booth engagement, virtual training, interactive design and other activities at events and exhibitions. (In the next section of this chapter I go into a lot more detail on the practical application of VR and AR that you can use to convert more business right now).

3. **Wearables**

These include smart watches, smart bracelets, smart name badges and wearable beacons.

This is a very exciting way to use technology to make an exhibition, event or, in particular, trade shows so much easier and more effective for everyone.

The Apple Watch has really fueled wearables as mainstream at events. They help to transform an attendee experience at tradeshows and events with a new level of convenience. We have all experienced the "fumble factor" of digging out phones from our pockets or purses to get the information we need.

Smart watches and other wearables help event participants to:

- Receive GPS directions.
- Receive directional indoor way-finding through a convention facility/exhibition hall.
- Open guestroom doors.
- Make e-wallet transactions that are faster and more secure than credit cards.
- Receive conference alerts and reminders of sessions.
- Exchange contact and lead retrieval information (and sync it with your Customer Relations Management (CRM)).
- Use as admission tickets.

- Make audience polling responses.
- Enable automated check-in for registration/meeting rooms.
- Record and track Continuing Education Unit (CEU) credits and much more.

The practical possibilities of this technology that I love is:

- Networking facilitation through taking a picture of whom you meet or face recognition reminders the next time you meet them.
- Note taking (video with sound and still picture recording on voice or touch demand).
- Displaying speaker presentation notes and slides.
- Mini-teleprompters for speakers.
- Site inspection facilitation to easily record meeting spaces.
- Social media interaction using video, geo-location and networking apps.

Hotels such as Starwood, Accor, InterContinental have apps for mobile check-in, arrival and departure information. Some feature loyalty points. Starwood allows guests to use the Apple Watch as a key to enter rooms at W Hotels, Aloft and Element properties.

Companies such as Loopd, AllianceTech, ITN, Limefy, Poken, TurnoutNow, XFocus are developing wearables beacons (often attached to or as part of a name badge) with many benefits: to assist in networking, contact exchange, way-finding, notifications, detailed crowd flow analytics, attendance tracking and more.

Detailed crowd flow analytics is a brilliant one for venues.

Imagine the operations team being able to see what buffet lines are the most popular and therefore need to be replenished?

4. Conference Event Guide and Multi-Event App Platforms for Larger Corporations and Associations

What is key about these technologies is the ability for the Planner to know what is happening on the event floor and be able to communicate that to the venue in real-time. It sharpens response times and keeps the event flowing as planned. Planners love that.

An app is almost standard at this point. Apps are being built for "Multi-events" for large corporations and associations. It is completely possible and would give a venue an edge to be able to offer this level of sophisticated technology to their conference and event clients.

Companies that are developing multi-event app platforms are:

Quickmobile.com, CrowdCompass.com, DoubleDutch.me, EventMobi.com, TripBuilderMedia.com, Certain.com, Core-Apps. Com, GenieConnect.com and Sherpa-solutions.com. Check them out, familiarize yourself with them as these technologies matter to your clients and to make an impact on the results achieved from a conference or event.

5. Mobile Social Networking

In previous chapters the importance of networking at a conference has been discussed. It is the number one reason many delegates attend a conference or event. To quote Ciara Feely, "I truly believe it is the venues responsibility to help facilitate this. One great contact can pay for the whole trip and ensure the delegate goes again next year. They walk out of the hotel buzzed and thinking very positive thoughts about the venue when they are delighted with the connections they made." For decades, the name badge was the principal networking tool. The networking plan was a little haphazard. Technology has and can greatly improve the networking process.

The combination of social media and technology is powerful for delivering events with greater outcomes for everyone – the Organizers, delegates and the venue. It is vital that hotels and venues be familiar with the importance of this and can facilitate it in every way. Partnerships can be formed with the major players in the industry as a strategy for converting more conference business.

Strong Wi-Fi is once again proving to be vital if a few hundred or a few thousand delegates will be accessing these apps at the event. Here are a few companies that have made a big impact on the networking process combining social media tools and mobile technology.

Bizzabo

Price: Free

Bizzabo is a business discovery app designed to help event organizers communicate with attendees and attendees with each other. Planners can add their event or import the details from Eventbrite - including logo, dates, times, place, social media links and agenda. A range of promotional tools is provided including "Download App" buttons and QR codes to include on your event website and promotional materials. There is an automatic scheduling function to send out notices to social media channels the weeks and days prior and during the event with customized reminders to download the app. Attendees can download the native app to be able to:

- See the conference agenda.

- See who else will be attending.

- Message fellow attendees.

- Set up face-to-face meetings onsite.

- Receive suggestions of business opportunities tailored to personal business profiles.

- Use LinkedIn to keep in touch with new connections.

- Use the Twitter event hashtag to be part of the buzz.

Shhmooze

Price: Free

Shhmooze is a smartphone app that matches a name, interests and expertise to the faces around you at a conference. Shhmooze highlights existing connections on LinkedIn and Twitter showing attendees whom they know and recommendations on who to meet.

Attendees sign into Shhmooze with LinkedIn, Twitter or Foursquare to create their profile. The app does not rely on the Conference Organizer to create the event.

These are just a few of the dozens of options out there. Most of the major event guide apps have built-in social media links as well. Many of the full-featured networking companies (such as Pathable.com, Presdo.com, DoubleDutch.me, Evenium.net) have strong mobile components.

When mobile technology and social media meet, the benefit is to create richer and more valuable events by helping attendees make the best connections possible.

6. **Marketing Power with Content Curator Tools Help Efficiently Manage Meetings Information and Interaction**

Information is cheap; knowledge is dear. This is where content curation is becoming essential. Content curation is the act of finding, grouping, organizing or sharing the best and most relevant content on a specific issue.

What is powerful about this technology is the marketing power it has for your venue. It allows the sales team to tell the story of client events at their venue. It is building real-life case studies on your clients that will help you to build relationships with Planners. It is social proof of what you can do in partnership with a Planner.

A smart way to use technology such as Conferize is to follow an event that has lost business, engage with the event/organizers and attendees while it is happening at your competitor's venue. However, most importantly build your portfolio of knowledge on this client so you know exactly what your pitch will be to secure next years' event.

There are millions of meetings each year creating massive amounts of data. This data, when organized and distributed properly, can be of significant value for review or to broadcast to a larger audience. It can also be very effective in promoting future events. Fortunately, there are tools to help with the information overload.

Eventifier.com collates all the event related contents from various social media streams like Twitter, YouTube, Instagram, Facebook, Flickr, Slideshare and many more. The event contents are archived and showcased in a dedicated, easy to use event page.

Conferize.com is a free social platform for discovering, following and attending conferences. It lets users follow conferences in real-time to find conversations, videos, presentations, photos and more. Users can be part of any conference community simply by chiming in or commenting specifically on content.

Storify.com allows users to "tell a story" by collecting media from across the web then publishing and sharing it on Storify and embedded on other websites.

Bundlr.com allows users to create topic pages with photos, videos, tweets and documents and then share them with everyone.

7. **Video and Images Dominate Social Channels and The Business Process for Events**

Events provide a great source of images and videos. The tools listed below will be used to increase attendee engagement and significantly broaden the social footprint of events.

Savvy users of **Twitter** know that a tweet with an image is nearly twice as likely to be retweeted. Similar statistics apply to other social channels. A variety of emerging social apps using photos, videos and video streaming are working their way into events.

Instagram is natural to use at events as it is inherently mobile. Twitter walls commonly include Instagram feeds as well as Twitter Images.

Snapchat has built a brand out of collecting photos and videos (four billion daily video views alone). It now offers "Live Stories" a curated stream of user submitted Snaps and videos from various locations and events. Users who have their location services on at the same event location will be given the option to contribute Snaps to the Live Story. The result is a story told from a community perspective with lots of different points of view.

This has massive marketing potential for event venues. For an example of this, check out Electric Daisy Carnival on YouTube.

Tradeshow and event **photo booths** are great for increasing attendee engagement, for capturing contact information and for broadening the impact of social media for events. They commonly post images (including the event hashtag) to Twitter, Instagram and/or Facebook. ChirpE, as an example, posts to Facebook and Twitter.

Look up **ChirpE** Photo Booth on YouTube for a great example of how to increase audience engagement, interaction and brand awareness at events. It is a fantastic idea to have on your stand at a trade show and create some buzz around your brand.

Videos are seeing an increasing usage at meetings. The Vine app allows users to post six-second videos and then share them to Twitter. When Facebook introduced auto-playing video in December 2013, the number of video posts jumped 75 percent that year.

8. **Streaming Video Apps (Another Great Way to Do a Virtual Site Inspection)**

Streaming video apps allow real-time video postings. They have become very common at events. Meerkat and Periscope are leading the way. Following Periscope's purchase by Twitter, ten million people registered for Periscope in just four months. More than forty years of video is watched each day. It is already a force to be reckoned with for events. Some Planners are struggling to figure out how to manage its use at sessions that may be confidential or covering sensitive subject matters. They also bring up copyright challenges.

They all lead to an absolute necessity for the venue to provide even greater Wi-Fi and cellular bandwidth usage. Video is getting cheaper and easier to produce. As video becomes omnipresent, we will see strong growth and reliance on it for event promotion and event content distribution. This can only be fantastic for hotels and venues marketing efforts as Planners can check out what a conference looks like and sounds like at a certain venue. It is also real content and valuable marketing material for the sales and marketing teams to share.

9. **Beacon Technology.**

This will be discussed in more detail in the next section. It has already had big impacts on events. This year's SXSW music/ technology conference in Austin deployed more than 1,000 beacons across some 265 venues in the city. Attendees used these beacons through the mobile app (provided by EventBase) for hyper-local networking – finding and knowing who was around you, event messaging based on location and much, much more.

DoubleDutch.me is using beacons with their app for a range of services including welcome notifications, directions, accurate in-room polling, networking and other options.

The San Diego Convention Center and the Boston Convention and Exhibition Center have deployed beacons throughout their facilities to assist in navigation and area information.

The Cisco Global Sale Experience issued beacon technology to measure crowd flow in food lines and transportation queues between the MGM Grand Garden Arena and the Mandalay Bay Convention Center for its 18,000 attendees.

10. **Deep Event Data Management and Customized Content Delivery**

Marketing Automation (MA) and CRM have been mature technologies in other sectors for some time. Finally, MA and advanced CRM tools are working their way into events.

Before the event: Attendee management companies are making much progress to customize the participant experience to drive more engagement and a richer experience. Companies such as Certain.com and Genie-Connect.com are linking MA and CRM technologies with registration data to capture and tie in rich attendee profiles. This helps to provide customized content and match-making for participants. Attendees, based on their profile, will receive customized promotional materials; content based on their interests and better suggested matches in a networking or appointment schedule. Cvent.com has built integration tools for Salesforce.com. Many attendee management software companies are linking social media channels as part of this process.

Onsite: Onsite has been referred to as the "black hole" of event data management. We have had tools for several years to manage basic participant information and logistics before and after the event, but not during it. Mobile event guide apps such as those provided by DoubleDutch.me and QuickMobile.com are changing this. It is possible for every touch on a mobile app to be tracked, scored and rated. Social media channels can be monitored and incorporated into the mix.

Onsite "likes" and surveys can be scored in real-time. Meeting Planners and event marketers can know immediately answers to the following questions: Who are the hot speakers, exhibitors, and influencers? What are the hot sessions, topics, and content? What is the buzz and what do the participants like or dislike? This immediate feedback is a goldmine of information to make midcourse corrections onsite and to engage participants with gamification and other audience engagement and recognition technologies. Feedback can be given immediately to the venue while the event is still taking place and they have the opportunity to address any issues attendees may have and ensure that happy delegates are walking out of the hotel or venue. This is a massive opportunity.

After the event: Onsite mobile data collected is also extremely valuable for designing and marketing future events.

11. Audience engagement becomes a top priority for events.

We are living in increasingly noisy times. We are being barraged with a daily "fire hose" of information that can be very daunting and is often tuned or filtered out. One benefit of meetings is that they take us away from our normal office environment to one where most of us feel a social contract to engage and be engaging with others. Meetings, when reduced to their most essential element, are about bringing people together.

However, there is much competition for our attention in our multi-media, socially-connected world. Traditional event paradigms of the "talking head" speaking to a passive audience, or a "build it and they will come" model for exhibitions are no longer acceptable. The word "attendee" is being replaced with "participant." Participants expect to be engaged. They expect to have a say in what is going on. They expect to continue to use their social media tools as they do at home. They expect to be treated as individuals rather than an email address on a mailing list. They are increasingly expecting a richer, more targeted and more interactive time at events, and are making their event purchasing choices accordingly.

Mobile social media and event apps are opening the door to a much more sensory and interactive experience and are fueling this transition. Gamification, the use of game thinking and game mechanics in a non-game context to engage users and solve problems, is seeing increased events and exhibition usage. Some consumer mobile apps such as Foursquare.com and SCVNGR.com have been used for this, but the trend is for more specialized event apps such as EventMobi.com, BoothTag. com, MeetingPlay.com. Larger mobile app developers such as DoubleDutch.me, QuickMobile.com, CrowdCompas.com, among others, are incorporating gaming into their larger event guide applications.

An engaged participant is a repeat participant and is one who will tell his or her colleagues as well.

Many of the twelve trends detailed here are involved in some way with participant engagement, a trend that is here to stay.

12. Second-screen Technology

Second-screen technology refers to the use of a mobile device to provide an enhanced viewing experience for other content usually with interactive features. This is seen most often on television, but increasingly so at events. Presenter content, such as slides, polling, video, notes, social media links, can be pushed to any device in real-time during a presentation.

13. Despite The Increased Use of Virtual Meetings Technology, Face-to-face Meetings and Tradeshows Will Remain Viable.

Virtual meeting, hybrid meeting and webinar usage are up. However, meetings and tradeshows continue to provide good value for your education, networking and sales budgets. Events offer unparalleled opportunities to bring buyers and sellers together, to build relationships, to brainstorm, to network. For an exhibitor, it is often the best way to meet so many qualified buyers in such a short time. For buyers, it is a great chance to meet vendors of interest – all together in one location, categorized and mapped for your choosing. The events, trade show and hospitality industries are relationship-based. Event and trade shows are some of the best ways to build these relationships.

Although webinars are good for short information exchange, meetings offer a much richer learning experience. What happens in the meeting room is important; people have made the commitment to be there and are not as distracted as in the office. However, the conversations in the hallways, receptions and exhibit hall contribute greatly to the information exchange.

Meetings provide a vastly richer, more targeted and more focused learning experience than any virtual meeting. There is no such thing as a "virtual beer!"

Corbin Ball, CMP, CSP is a speaker and independent third party consultant focusing on meetings technology. With twenty years of experience running international citywide technology meetings, he now helps clients worldwide use technology to save time and improve productivity. He can be contacted at his extensive web site:
www.corbinball.com
www.twitter.com/corbinball

For my part, I think the **smartest marketing technology** a venue can provide is a *Charging Station*. Everyone has a smartphone or device that needs constant charging when in use at events. The charger is a most commonly forgotten item at home and indeed left behind in the hotel guestroom. Hotels that are providing this service at an event will be looked upon as a savior! You know that sense of relief you get when you find a free plug to charge the phone, tablet or laptop at. Investing in a Charging Station would be a wise decision. It will guarantee positive word of mouth as it is the little things like that that make a delegate's life easy. It is an opportunity to engage with delegates and get great feedback on the event if positioned properly.

Technology for Venues to help WIN more Conference and Event Business

By Brandt Krueger; Contributing Author.

The Right Technology at the Right Price

Because the technology landscape is always shifting, it can be difficult for venues to decide what, if any, of the latest trends to put their money behind. Nobody wants to sink large amounts of money into a product that likely won't be around in five years.

At the same time, customers (especially those under thirty) are looking for a certain amount of technological sophistication from their venues and keep a keen eye on which venues are moving forward with advancements in technology. While there are obvious infrastructure enhancements that can be made, such as Wi-Fi, power and installing charging stations, there are plenty of other technology trends that can be harnessed by the tech-savvy venue. The only question is how much will they cost and how much of a perceived value will there be for potential customers?

What follows are a few technologies that I not only believe

deliver the biggest bang for the buck when it comes to meeting and event technology but specifically ones that venues can own, maintain and install themselves.

Projection Mapping

Projection and display technology is one of the most cost-effective, impactful and emotionally inspiring ways we can spice up our events.

We have all seen spectacular examples of big brands telling their story by projection mapping onto iconic surfaces such as the Sydney Opera House, The Roman Colosseum and even most recently on the Hoover Dam. Many people do not realize, however, that it can be done on a very simple, yet effective level within a hotel or venue that adds the WOW factor to an event. Indeed, some venues have already started to leverage the power of projection in creative, customizable and low cost ways.

The Imagineers at Disney were among the first that I noticed taking projection mapping and bringing it down to a smaller scale for events (It is a small world, after all). In late 2014, they announced as part of their wedding packages the ability to project customized animations featuring Disney characters:

"With wedding cake animation that scrolls over icing like a mini movie, Disney desserts can now be transformed with fully customizable image mapping projection technology. Whether you want to showcase a photo slideshow, home video or your favorite quote, fondant is refashioned into an enchanted animated canvas that is sure to impress."

This is not some high-tech effect that costs thousands of dollars;

it's a white cake being projected on by one or two projectors, combined with a little creativity and animation. This type of effect can be achieved with off-the-shelf technology and could easily be applied to other aspects of a party or event, including bars, ice sculptures and lounge furniture. The surface just has to be mostly white.

Cost effective Projection Mapping

If you are concerned about the expense of creating full motion animation, there are plenty of stock video and image sites that have beautiful, high-definition photos and videos available. I have seen compelling projection being done using textures and color built into a PowerPoint presentation. It can all be done with stock video, or the client will have their branded photos and videos to project.

It is your role as the venue to give them ideas on how to make their event more impactful. The more you are helping them to run an amazing event, the more you are aligning yourself as a partner and winning more business. Projection Mapping is just one simple techy way to do this.

WIN More Events Using Technology

A room can be transformed and given a completely different evening look by using white surfaces and projecting an image onto them. If you find Planners are not booking their evening events at your hotel as they want a different look and feel for the event, this is a solution to present to them. Turn a boring couch into a colorful, inviting place for guests to relax - you can even project an image of a roaring fire on the wall beside them. Images can be projected onto a white wall or onto white table cloths to transform a room from day conference to WOW awards or gala event. All without the expense of renting new furniture or big production companies.

Projection Mapping is an extremely low cost, high impact add-on for almost any event.

Virtual/Augmented Reality

Virtual Reality (VR) and Augmented Reality (AR) have been on a lot of people's "What to watch for" lists for years, but it was not until around 2015 that things started to take off in both fields.

First off, a quick break for definitions, specifically the difference between VR and AR.

AR is the process of layering something *over* reality. Whether on your smartphone or in some kind of headset, the observer can still see the world around them in the device and the content is layered over that world.

VR involves going all the way down the rabbit hole and is meant to be an immersive experience. The world around the observer is replaced by a virtual one. An example of AR would be Google Glass, and an example of VR would be Oculus Rift or Google Cardboard. Although many believe that AR has a strong future, it is VR that is seen the most growth in recent years.

Consumer VR headsets of every size, shape and price range have been introduced. Google Cardboard, which was a VR viewer so low cost it was made out of, you guessed it, cardboard. While much attention has been paid to high-end VR systems such as Oculus Rift, it was Google Cardboard that made me realize that VR had finally come of age. Here was a VR viewer that was such low cost it could be handed out at a trade show booth and anyone with a modern smartphone could insert it into the unit for a fairly compelling VR experience.

It is one thing to hand someone a brochure with a bunch of photos; it is quite another to give them access to three-dimensional, fully 360° views. Imagine a potential guest putting on a headset and a pair of headphones, so they could not only see the panoramic views offered by your seaside location but also hear the waves crashing and birds calling. Imagine them not only being able to see your ballroom but also being able to see it from different angles, in different configurations and with different decor. It is a very powerful tool to use to help bring your venue to a client. Initial contact with a client generally involves you visiting their office, instead of showing the client flat 2D photos the cardboard Google View can be used to make them feel like they are standing in your hotel lobby or ballroom. Your role as a salesperson is to help the Planner visualize their event at your hotel or venue. This is a serious tool to help you do that.

What's the cost of this technology?
Google Cardboard Viewer $20
360° HD Camera $500+

A few venues and destinations have begun to experiment with the power of VR as a marketing tool, but why aren't more of them? There is a perception out there that this technology must still be years away, or at the very least, must cost a fortune to record. Not true. The technology is here and viewing devices are very affordable. Even the cameras to help you create the visuals for these technologies are now within the budget. High-definition, 360-degree cameras are available for under $500.

For a minimal investment, venues are now quite capable of generating these immersive videos themselves, which can be posted directly to YouTube and played back on any compatible VR viewer. Hotels can even distribute custom-branded versions of Google Cardboard with their marketing materials for less than some print companies charge for high-end photo brochures.

They are a very powerful tool to use to get the Planner interested in coming to take a look for themselves at your hotel or venue.

Imagine sending a Google Cardboard presentation along with a proposal to a client - that would help to get your proposal to the top of the pile of venues being considered.

The time to get into the VR game is now before the market becomes saturated as savvy venues are starting to jump in with both feet.

AR as a Marketing Tool

What about AR? The pace of progress has been much slower in the field of AR, with Google Glass getting much initial hype, but then quietly fading into the background. Nonetheless, AR is something venues need to keep an eye on. Much like VR, the cost of AR technology is going to come down rapidly and may also quickly become an indispensable marketing tool. Unlike its counterpart, AR technology is more likely to be an exclusively "on property" tool.

Imagine once more that you would like to show off your main conference room, only, this time, your potential client is visiting on a full site inspection. If you have ever had the experience of your main conference room being in use the day a big potential client comes in for a show around, this is one effective way around that problem.

With the power of AR, a potential client could stand in the middle of the conference room (or outside it if it is in use) and look through AR goggles, see the world as it is - a big empty room. With the flick of a switch, the AR goggles could overlay different seating configurations and show what the room looks like set for a corporate meeting, theatre style, cabaret, or how it might look set up for a gala event. You can have powerful conversations in the room with the client, helping them to imagine their event happening in your conference room. The best time to overcome objections is when the client is there with you in the event room. This technology will assist you to have deeper level conversations with the client. Moreover, have them walking out, imagining their event running smoothly at your venue.

AR as a Navigation Tool at an Exhibition
Another potential AR use case comes in the form of navigation. Imagine being handed a set of AR glasses as part of the check- in process for an expo. Using the event app, you could look up a vendor's booth number, but instead of trying to find it on the massive map of the show floor, a beacon, flag, or arrow is placed in your glasses to show you where it is on the floor, and how far away it is. Arrows appear on the carpet below indicating the fastest way to get to the booth.

Beacons and Intralocation Systems

What GPS did for navigating around the world, Intralocation (inside or indoor location) technologies are doing for navigation on the small-scale. Being able to locate a person precisely inside a building, or even just on the resort property can be tremendously valuable to a guest, as well as to the Meeting or Event Planner.

There are several kinds of technologies available to assist in intralocation. The most often written about are **beacons**. Beacons are tiny devices that use a low-energy form of Bluetooth radio to communicate with devices such as smartphones, tablets, and other devices. They can range in size from about the size of a postage stamp to about the size of a fist, depending on their range and battery size. They can be stuck onto a wall, placed in a tradeshow booth, or set up strategically throughout an event space.

You may hear them referred to as "iBeacons," which is the term Apple chose to brand its version of the protocol, but Apple has not released its beacon hardware. It was brilliant marketing to get the name out there early, but there is no such thing as "an iBeacon" yet.

While the initial buzz surrounding beacons seemed to focus on location-aware notifications (i.e. walking by a clothing store pops up a "Pants! 35% OFF!" notification on your smartphone), the real benefit from beacons has come in the form of intralocation. Because beacons use radio technology, it is relatively easy to triangulate a person's location using multiple beacons.

The Benefits of Tracking the Movement of Attendees

Beyond beacons, others have successfully used Wi-Fi radio signals to track the movements of attendees. Again, initially invented as a way to track shoppers as they moved through the store, this technology was adapted to provide tracking at events and expos, with some degree of success.

This newest way of using beacons to track attendees is by having a battery-powered beacon clipped into the attendee's lanyard, kept in their pocket or worn. The beacon detectors around the event space can then triangulate the position of each device.

This generates a tremendous amount of data for Conference Planners to analyze, not only after the fact but also in real-time. Through this technology, Planners can see a visualization of their event space, including all activities, photo stations, bars or expo booths. Overlaid on that map is a triangle or dot representing each attendee as they move around. A Planner could see in real-time that the lines at bars one and two are backing up and blocking the door, so it might be time to open up bars three and four ahead of schedule.

These visualizations can provide far more accurate detail as to which parts of the event were a hit, or more importantly, which flopped. Just because the two times an organizer peeked in the room the Vodka Luge was packed, doesn't mean it was that way the whole night and the technology could help determine if it was worth the money it cost to bring it in. It also means the Planner and venue management can show expo exhibitors exactly the kind of traffic they are likely to see on aisle 200 of the show floor vs. aisle 700, justifying the increased cost of booths in that section.

Facilities too can benefit from the analysis of these traffic patterns, gaining insight on catering stations and bar locations for example. What works, what doesn't and what causes backups can make the difference between a perfect event and a near miss.

These are powerful insights for a venue to use to help them win more big events and more lucrative business. It also immediately demonstrates that you understand their world and that you have solutions ready to overcome the big challenges they have in running their events.

Using Beacons to Increase the Revenue Spend Per Guest

The possibilities for integrating with mobile apps (and maybe soon AR) allows guests to easily find their way around the venue.

I cannot tell you the number of times I have certainly wished for *turn by turn* navigation inside some resort properties! And while I loathe the idea of getting more pop-up notifications, a few well-placed signals might be nice, such as, "by the way, there is a table open by the fireplace in the bar you're now walking past," or "a slot just opened up on the tour that departs within 100 meters of you." If the notification is infrequent and importantly is *opt-in*, that kind of notification is an opportunity to help increase the revenue spend per guest at your venue.

These benefits - guest location, Planner insights, and venue insights - make intralocation a powerful *triple threat* of event technology and a compelling up-sell for potential group business. Check out Loopd as a great example of wearable beacons.

Conclusions: These are just a few of the many technology innovations that are helping venues to sell more effectively and convert more leads. Tech-forward venues are already starting to provide these services and many others in an attempt to attract younger, more tech-savvy guests and Planners. As prices on these technologies continue to fall, more and more will begin to use them as part of their sales and marketing to the lucrative conference and event market.

Now is the time to experiment with what works for your property. It means you will not be trying to play catch up as your competitors move into the future without you!

Brandt Krueger is a Consultant, Meeting and Event Technology Instructor and speaker. A content creator for the Event Leadership Institute and podcaster on GatherGeeks – a podcast by BizBash.
www.BrandtKrueger.com

Virtual Site Inspections

Technology to help the Planner visualize their event at your Venue

We touched on Virtual Reality in the Conference Technology section. This section is my interpretation of how venues can practically apply this technology to help them convert more leads and help get more Planners to their venue. I consulted with James Corbett of Simvirtua as the technology expert on this one.

It is harder and harder to get to the site inspection step of the buying process. Planners have to be convinced that your property is a right fit for their event before they will take the time to visit your property.

One way to reassure them that their time will not be wasted is to bring the venue to them. With VR you can step into a space without actually being there. There are a number of ways to do this. I find Google Cardboard is one of the easier and least expensive ways.

How Google Cardboard Can Help You Convert More Business

By James Corbett of SimVirtua; Contributing Author.

So what is Google Cardboard? It is a special headset, worn over the eyes, which looks like goggles made from cardboard. There is a slot at the front that fits your phone. An app is downloaded to the phone; the phone fits into the front of the headset, and your venue is brought to the Planner, in 3D video format, right from the comfort of their office. They literally feel like they are walking around your property.

The cardboard goggles can be branded and presented in different colors. A QR code (this looks like a barcode) is printed on the cardboard that when scanned directs the Planner to the app you want them to download. That app is the virtual tour of your venue. They then put their phone in the front of the Google Cardboard and virtually experience your venue.

When the Planner wearing the headset moves their head the 3D image on the internal display changes as it would if they were looking at the real world view of your venue. This creates a convincing illusion of being in your lobby or conference room.

The advantage of Virtual Reality over photo galleries and video is that our human brains have evolved a natural talent for interpreting and remembering three-dimensional spaces while we struggle to reassemble a collection of photographs (e.g. from a photo gallery) into a cohesive whole. It is said that a picture is worth a thousand words and a video is worth a thousand pictures. We can now also say a Virtual Reality is worth a thousand videos.

Convert More Leads Using Technology

It is a very powerful way to present a proposal to a Planner – clients so rarely receive anything fun and interesting in the post these days. By sending the proposal printed out with the Google Cardboard and instructions on how to use it is a sure way to ensure you get the client's interest. This helps to position your venue in the top 10 percent of venues being considered.

This is also very powerful technology to use at industry trade shows or on sales calls. The Google Cardboard viewer specification is open source which means there are many manufacturers of the kits. In bulk, they can be purchased for less than $20 each.

Benefits

These Virtual Reality tours of your venue can also have audio on them. You can also personalize tours for different clients and lead them through your venue as if they were there with you. The benefits of them being able to pause their tour, stand in the conference room, get a feel for the room, look up at the ceiling, experience the sense of space in the room, see where the projector is and walk through the exhibition space (which you can have set up or not), immediately proves how client and conference centric your venue is.

The Planner can get a sense of the flow from place to place, the proportions of spaces and the connections between rooms and even walk outside and experience your venue as their delegates would arriving at their event.

In essence, VR allows one to **visit** a place again and again without ever going there in person. Moreover, to **remember** a space in great detail without ever having been there. The benefits of this for a committee of people who are trying to decide on a venue when perhaps one or two members have visited the location are very exciting. When a venue is helping potential clients to visualize their event at a venue, you are making it so easy for them to buy from you. That is what Planners love – making it easy to work with you.

What Does It Involve to Create Your Own Virtual Reality Demo?

For the venue: To create the Virtual Reality app a full survey of the target areas, both inside and outside the hotel, must be undertaken. This involves the recording of measurements, photographs, video, and audio. Access to existing floor plans and building blueprints can allow the model to be created with greater speed and accuracy.

Options for the finished app include the following.

- Audio: A voiceover narration can guide the Planner through the VR. That narration can be:

(a) Linear- where progression is from start to finish without interruption.

(b) Interactive- where the Planner triggers audio elements corresponding to where they are in the VR.

- Navigation: The progression of movement through the VR can be:

(a) Point to point- where the Planner is automatically moved from location to location after a set period of time and has the freedom to look all around them from a stationary point at each interval.

(b) Rail-tracked- where the Planner is taken on a guided tour as if sitting on a slowly moving train carriage that traces a predetermined path around the facility at a set speed.

(c) Full freedom; where the Planner can move anywhere in the VR at their pace.

Planners: The basic requirement to view the Virtual Reality app is a smartphone and Google Cardboard headset. The smartphone should be mid-range or better and two years old or newer to provide a comfortable experience. The Planner launches the app on the phone then places it in the headset. Note, it is best experienced when sitting down as the motion can make some people a little light-headed.

Check out how real estate firm, Sherry Fitzgerald use this technology to sell houses off plans.

For more information on this technology and to speak to an expert on how you can create this for your venue, contact **James Corbett** of Simvirtua.
www.Simvirtua.com

Action Items from This Section:

Connect with James Corbett on www.Simvirtua.com
Connect with Brandt Krueger on www.BrandtKrueger.com
Connect with Corbin Ball on www.corbinball.com

Wi-Fi

Being up to speed on your Wi-Fi and Bandwidth Speed is an important part of your Tech Toolkit, to help you WIN!

Understanding bandwidth and Wi-Fi capacity is just as important as knowing the capacity of your conference rooms according to Ruth Hill who prepared a white paper on this topic. If you stumble when answering questions in this area, it will say to the client that you do not do many of their type of event and make the client a little nervous of booking with you.

A conversation about Wi-Fi and bandwidth is an important one to have early in their decision-making process. I know it can be hard to have that all-important conversation. If you make it to the site tour step, it is vital to explore Wi-Fi in detail and even do a demo on the site tour to prove your capacity. It is essential to have this conversation at the point in the Planner's buying process when you know you are being seriously considered.

Having the answers straight off to the following questions will immediately build trust and confidence with the Planner that your team has the expertise to deliver their event.

- How many wireless devices can the network support?

- Is the Wi-Fi shared or is it possible to get dedicated Wi-Fi for an event?

- What is the bandwidth in the property's meeting facilities, at what point does that max out?

- What is the bandwidth for the sleeping rooms, at what occupancy does that max out?

- What is the Wi-Fi coverage in the common areas – lobby, bar, restaurant?

This is an important conversation to have upfront with the Planner. There is nothing worse than you discovering a few days before an event that there are bandwidth issues, it will cause a big panic and the venue may end up having to cover the bill.

I would advise creating a separate document you can simply send on to prospective clients and indeed have it available as a download from your website. I suggest you write down every question you have been asked about Wi-Fi and put them in this document. When you have immediate answers to these questions, you are building trust and confidence that your team has the required expertise.

A great resource is the Convention Industry Council APEX Standards Committee Bandwidth Estimator*. You can immediately confirm if your bandwidth is strong enough to handle the requirements of a Planner. Send this on to your clients so they can check themselves and book with confidence. It is much better for them to know in advance if they have to pay to pump up the bandwidth capacity than it becomes an unplanned expense once the contract is signed.

** The Convention Industry Council, HSMAI, and APEX have put together a very detailed white paper which outlines how Event Planners and venues should plan for their Wi-Fi usage. I have summarized it in the following paragraphs:

What is the *event or meeting's bandwidth demand?* What is the expected level of internet usage onsite? This should include the number and types of mobile devices in use such as smartphones, tablet and laptops and e-readers.

What do presenters and facilitators require for such functions as live demos, app training and remote collaboration? How much (low, med, high) bandwidth is required?

Consider exhibitors' private wireless networks. Their Wi-Fi equipment can interfere with a venue's bandwidth network. Too many wireless networks too close together can cause interference that causes all to stall or shut down.

Know whether the event requires *shared or dedicated bandwidth.* Shared bandwidth means everyone in a venue may be competing for capacity, but it may be satisfactory for casual use like checking email and systems not critical for the event. Dedicated bandwidth is set aside and guaranteed for a specific use such as a keynote presentation. It is recommended for large events, presenter networks, hybrid meeting activities, and critical event operating systems.

Know what the property's network service provider is capable of? Can they offer dedicated bandwidth for individual groups? What is the pricing for dedicated bandwidth?

The availability, access, and pricing for dedicated bandwidth is information that you should not only know but stay up to date on, since technology changes rapidly, and infrastructure improvements can happen quickly.

Know the bandwidth of the *property's meeting facilities*. At what point does that max out? If this is a group that pushes the property's physical capacity, you need to know if there is enough bandwidth to support all those maxed-out meeting rooms and if the Wi-Fi network can handle all the devices in those rooms. If not, you will need to talk about ways to supplement the Wi-Fi or bring in bandwidth and the costs involved in both. The property's network service provider is crucial in this conversation.

Question what the event apps need to do. Do apps store schedules and other information, or do they pull them from the internet each time they are accessed? Do they use photo or video uploading? Is there gamification that requires check-ins, social media interaction, photo scavenger hunts, and so on? An app provider should be able to estimate how much bandwidth can be required.

I would advise that you yourself verify the bandwidth in the main conference room or meeting room area. You could lose a sale if on a site tour the Planner checked it, and it was not what you had advised it would be. You can check available speed against on verification sites like www.speedtest.net and www.speakeasy.net/speedtest.

Ask about the *group's past experiences*. Have they had service or capacity issues? This can be a real emotional issue for a client, especially if they have had an embarrassing experience in the past with it. It can give you **the edge** by really understanding their need and know how to overcome that problem for them.

Knowing what has caused problems before can help the property's network service provider make the right recommendations about what type of service that will avoid repeating these problems. This may be an opportunity to talk about dedicated bandwidth and Wi-Fi capacity.

What is the *bandwidth for the sleeping rooms*, at what occupancy does that max out? Guest room internet access has been identified as one of the key satisfaction indicators for both frequent travelers and meeting attendees. Understanding where a property's occupancy level can affect guest room bandwidth is important, especially with large groups and during high-occupancy periods.

Be familiar with what's offered in common areas. Very often properties offer internet service in public space and food outlets, sometimes for free, but often this service offers very limited bandwidth suitable for email and simple browsing by a few people only. It is important to set the correct expectation with the client about the level of bandwidth and Wi-Fi capacity available in this area.

Connect the Planner with the hotel's event technology experts. They should know who they can turn to at the property for more information, additional guidance and technical expertise; whether that is an in-house expert or someone who manages the hotel's relationship with the network service provider. With technology and infrastructure investment continuing to evolve at an increasing pace, you cannot assume past information is still accurate.

Refer to the IT expert for questions such as:
Does the property have a big enough pipe (total bandwidth coming to a property) to provide our overall bandwidth needs? Can your property set up sub-separate networks (VLANs-Virtual Local Area Network) for every need?

Action Items from This Section:

- Create a document on your Wi-Fi capacity to share on your website and with the sales and operations teams.

- Ensure you can answer all the questions raised in this section. Knowing and being very clear and upfront about your Wi-Fi capabilities is a key area to build trust and confidence with the Planner.

- The Convention Industry Council (CIC), HSMAI & APEX have produced some brilliant research conducted on the industry. The source article was a white paper prepared by Ruth Hill, "Getting Up to Speed on Event Bandwidth."

What are my top learnings so far?

WONDERFUL
OPPORTUNITY
TO WIN

WOW

Step 3

Proposals that WIN!

"I went from chasing a corporate client for 3 years and not winning the business, to converting 75% of the Meeting & Conference Business for this year."

Heather Thornton, Director of Sales of Six Properties With Yew Lodge Business Solutions, Birmingham, UK.

Yes, Heather went from 0% to 75% conversion rate with a client after working with me. She used a few of these techniques that Andy shares in this chapter. This is **Step 3** in my **7 Steps System**. It is so important it gets a step all by itself.

How to Write Proposals that WIN!

My first job was as a sales coordinator for five hotels in San Francisco. I worked with two Senior Sales Managers and I spent all day every day just sending out proposals. My focus was on getting the proposal done and off my desk and sent to the client. I did not focus on or ask, what would convert the business? That should have been my priority! When I became the client, I realized the standard of proposals in the industry. I saw exactly why business was being lost. Most Directors of Sales will say to me that they are happy with their proposal. Perhaps they recently revamped it or invested in e-proposal software. However, when I read it, I realize that it is all about the property. We need to switch that around and make it all about the client.

I spoke with Deborah Gardner, a performance expert. She made a strong analogy that the early steps of engaging with a client is a little like dating. You have to make an impression, captivate them, you have to WOW them and pull them in. You have to make them want a second date. Andy shows us how to do this in the all-important proposal.

Most proposals in any industry make that classic mistake. The client does not care about your property, they only care about their problems. (adapted from a saying by Marshal Goldsmith) So we must address these problems in the proposal.

Andy Bounds has had a big impact on my business. I call him the "AFTERs" man. His insights have helped me to develop my perspective and teach hotels how to win more. For that reason, I asked him to contribute this chapter to my book on "**How to Write Proposals That WIN!**" When this technique is applied to your business it works.

The ABC Method: The Easiest Way to Generate Sales

By Andy Bounds; Contributing Author.

When selling, only one thing matters:

Delight the customer so much that they want to give you their money.

And what is the easiest way to master how to delight a customer? Simply think what delights you when you are a customer...and make sure you do it when selling to others!

ABC – The Only Three Things a Customer Wants

Imagine you are the customer, buying a website. There are only three things you need when choosing between different website companies. And that is for the website company to:

- Establish what outcomes you want the website to deliver –

generating leads, raising profile, annoying the competition, etc.

- Then prove they can build a website which will deliver these outcomes for you.

- Then give you a couple of options for you to choose between – different price points, different color schemes and the like. After all, it's better to have some choice than no choice.

You can rewrite these three steps using what I call ABC.

- **AFTERs:** where you want to be AFTER working with the supplier.

- **Build certainty:** the supplier proves they can give you these AFTERs.

- **Choice:** they offer you 2-3 options as to how you accept their proposal.

And, of course, this isn't just the case with websites. Imagine installing a new IT system in your company, you'd want the IT company to:

- **AFTERs:** identify what you want your company to look like AFTER installing the new system.

- **Build certainty:** prove that your company will look like this after their involvement.

- **Choice:** give you a couple of ways you can get the IT system you want.

Or, going to an optician and buying glasses?

- **AFTERs:** see better, look trendy, impress the opposite sex.

- **Build certainty:** let you try on various pairs, so you can see which look right on you.

- **Choice:** whittle it down to 2-3 options, for you to choose between.

You'll notice with all these examples – and I could have given you hundreds more – that the key is to find the AFTERs first. After all, unless the supplier knows what improved future you want, how can you/they know they can deliver it for you?

Sounds obvious, yes?

Well, yes... in theory. But it goes against what most salespeople do in practice. Instead of talking about the customer's future, they tend to talk about their own past; "Founded in 1922," "Look at a map of all our venues" and so on.

So, the bad news is most salespeople focus on the wrong thing. But the great news for you is if you change, you suddenly become better than the competition. Result! And here's how to do it...

Mastering Selling - It's as Easy as ABC

As you'd expect, the three steps of mastering ABC are... well, to master each of the three steps of A, B, and C. In other words:

- **AFTERs: know all the AFTERs that you deliver, and also good questions to uncover the ones most relevant to a particular customer.**

- **Build certainty: know the best ways to prove you can deliver each of the AFTERs, so you bring these out in your sales meetings.**

- **Choice: have 2-3 options you can offer, so the customer stops thinking "Do I buy?" and starts thinking "Which do I buy?"**

Mastering the A

There are two steps here:

1. Be aware of all the AFTERs that you deliver.

2. Know the best questions to ask, to uncover the most relevant ones.

Taking each in turn...

Start by *identifying* all the AFTERs that you feel customers can get from you. Here is a list to kick things off for you:

• Participants to feel they are very well taken care of.

• Networking – it is essential that it is easy for the delegates to meet, have conversations and mingle.

• Be recognized as the expert they are in their topic.

• Delegates to learn and stay up to date with the latest trends in the industry.

Secondly script *in advance of the meeting* good questions to ask, to uncover which of these AFTERs are their priorities. Good questions to ask include:

• What are you looking to achieve from your conference?

• What do you want your boss/the committee to feedback to you after the event?

• What if anything would you change about last year's event or indeed previous events?

Mastering the B

Once you know all the AFTERs you can deliver, the next step is to know (again, *in advance*) how you're going to prove you can deliver them. Usually, this will be one or more of the following:

- Case studies where you delivered similar AFTERs for other customers previously.
- Testimonials describing the AFTERs that you delivered.
- A list of customers to whom you have delivered similar AFTERs.
- Free advice about how they can get their AFTERs (nothing transmits your expertise more than you teaching people ideas they didn't know they didn't know).

Here is a very useful exercise: Copy your list of AFTERs from before into the left-hand column, and list 3-4 proofs showing your ability to deliver each on the right, e.g.:

AFTERs... the customer wants	Proofs... I can deliver it.
Delegates to feel they are very well taken care of	➢ Testimonial from a similar client stating this. ➢ Testimonial from a delegate stating this; ideally a video of them while still at your venue. ➢ Share what the staff ratio would be for the event.

Mastering the C

Once you've proved you can deliver the AFTERs they want, finish by offering them a couple of choices as to how they get them.

Salespeople often forget to do this. In effect, they say, "We can definitely help you. It will cost £5,000. Do you want to go ahead or not?" So that often can lead to the answer "not."

Instead, a better close is to say: "We can definitely help you. And there are two ways we can do so. The better and therefore more expensive option is to do X which will cost £X. Or we could remove a couple of elements from it, taking it down to Y, which will cost £Y. Which of those do you prefer?" By adding in a third option, you help to narrow down the choice again, generally, you will find most people will go for the middle range option.

Again, a very useful exercise to do is to list a few options that you could offer. Use the following as a guide:

The Basic Package:

Tea/coffee, regular biscuits. Soup and Sandwiches lunch, room rental, standard guestroom.

All are standards you will not go below, but are happy to get these rates.

The Medium Package:

This will include upgrades and have more of an emphasis on nourishing the delegates, brain food, extra audiovisuals.

Small Upgrade:

On the tea/coffee breaks, tea/coffee on arrival, hot lunch, room rental, standard guestroom and a few upgrades, dinner options, drinks reception.

The Gold Option Package:

This package includes your top end food and beverage options all carefully selected by the chef, personalized menus, a consultation with the chef as well as additional services listed below (which can be outsourced). These must be discussed with the client in advance to ensure they are of value to them.

- Registration service (staff to help out with the conference).

- Printing Service (so they don't have to bring all of the materials).

- Signage.

- Photographer.

- Off-Site Event.

ABC – Putting It All Together

Once you have each of the three in place...

- **AFTERs:** a list of all the ones you offer, plus the best questions to establish where the customer's priorities lie

- **Build certainty:** a list of the best proofs for each one of the

AFTERs

- **Choice:** 2-3 options for each one of these AFTERs

- ...selling becomes much more straightforward, in that you:

- **Ask questions** to find what their AFTERs are

- **Build certainty** to prove that you can *deliver* them

- **Offer** them a couple of *choices* as to how they accept again and again and again...
  ... And that's my favorite sort of technique – maximum sales for minimal effort!

The best way to know what to put in the proposal is to ask your clients. Send them exactly what will help them to say **YES**.

And if you would like more AFTERs from Andy...

There are two other ways I can help you AFTER reading this section. The first is free, the second isn't. (Once again...always offer a choice!)

Action Items from This Section:

- Tuesday Tips: My free, weekly emails containing sales/ communication best practices.

- Sign up at: www.andybounds.com/tips

- My monthly videos: One hour every month, with me providing simple, practical advice that you can watch on your computer, and then implement immediately.

Find out more at: www.andyboundsonline.com

I highly recommend Andy and the power of taking his approach with your business. I have certainly learned a lot from his practical wisdom.

What are my top learnings so far?

WONDERFUL
OPPORTUNITY
TO WIN

WOW

Perfect Fit Planner™

"Opened up a whole new market!

Ciara helped us to open a whole new market segment that we hadn't considered possible for our hotel. We converted two conferences within a few weeks of applying her advice and tips. She just made it easy."

Tara Cronin, Vienna Woods Hotel, Cork, Ireland.

Identifying The Perfect Fit Planner™

Profiling Your Ideal Clients

OK, so up to now I have shown you how to build the right Sales and Marketing Tools for your target market. What is vital however is to ensure you are building these tools for the right kind of clients – the clients that are a perfect fit for your property. I call them the **Perfect Fit Planner™**.

Start with writing down who is your best client – the most profitable business you have ever booked. A client that was a pleasure to work with, was a perfect fit for the property; consider the ease of operations, how it all flowed, the great reviews you got and the testimonials. Start there. Work backwards. I have put together a cheat sheet to help you profile this client and go into detail. Print out the **Perfect Fit Planner™** Profile Checklist and bring to your next sales meeting to brainstorm with your colleagues. I will give you the download link at the end of this chapter.

To build a rich picture of who you serve, you have got to understand your ideal client's wants, needs, thoughts and fears in intimate detail.

Why? Because it will make it much easier to find them and to attract leads and interest from them. When you are speaking their language and are clear about who you are looking for, it is a lot easier to find more of your perfect type of client.

There are a number of attributes top performing salespeople have in common. A big one is that they all have a target list of clients, and they work consistently from that list. Ideally, you should always have a list of twenty people you are looking to connect with; whose business you have identified as a perfect fit for your property. To help you come up with that list, I have created a profile checklist that you can download from this link:

www.ConferenceConverter.com/bookresources

When you are clear about whom you need to speak with, my guest author in this section, Amy Infante,has some brilliant tips on how to reach that person and get a conversation with them. The level of client research Amy goes into will help you gain an even bigger understanding of your client – before you contact them. Amy Infante, and her team at Plan B Consultants, devised a system on how to master the art of prospecting; a valuable skill to command.

Finding More of the Right Clients

By Amy Infante of Plan B Consultants; Contributing Author.

To say that it is difficult to capture the attention of decision-makers in our industry is a gross understatement. I am often the sounding board for hotel owners and sales leadership venting about their frustration over the fact that their sales team just can't catch the attention of those target customers. Not only is the leadership frustrated, but hotel Sales Managers around the world are feeling inadequate, frustrated and demeaned by customers that will not give them the time of day. The sales cycle for gaining target accounts is long and painful. This obviously leads to failure in hitting sales targets, which turns into frustration for owners and hotel leadership wondering if they have the proper sales team in place, the proper sales deployment and the proper goals. Ultimately this vicious cycle leads to high turnover.

When a sales person feels inadequate at selling and has a challenge with one of the fundamentals of sales (capturing the attention of and getting face-time with a customer), then the extreme happens. Sales teams crumble either by force or by nature because they are not able to do their job. To understand this phenomenon, that truly is a mainstream issue affecting all hotel sales professionals whether they are representing a mid- scale, extended stay, boutique or luxury resort, we must dive into some key challenges. Once we understand the busy decision-maker and their challenges, we can better examine some key ways to break through the clutter, capture their interest and ultimately win more sales.

The Challenge

Over the past several years, automation has taken over the industry. With a push of a button, anyone can send a lead to any hotel around the world and expect a response within hours with rates, dates and space. From the decision-maker's perspective, there is no reason for face-to-face meetings, site tours or even a phone call. Online virtual tours of hotels are set up. We have entire websites devoted to reviews of guest experiences at hotels. Decision-makers can shop competitor rates and your hotel's best available rate through the various online travel agencies to ensure they are getting the best deal.

It can all be handled electronically to save time and energy. Those in charge of meetings and travel do not need to field hundreds of phone calls from eager hotel Sales Managers. They can automate the process and cut back on time. Nine times out of ten planning meetings and arranging travel are just a portion of their job duties. If they do not have time to develop a personal relationship with their vendors, why bother? They can trust the systems that are in place and make a decision from the overload of information gathered via the systems that have been built to manage time, cut costs and maximize efficiency.

In many respects, the hospitality industry has supported this automation and even embraced it. Technology provides tracking and measuring to ensure things do not fall through the cracks. Proposals can be tracked more efficiently; customer information is more easily stored; sales teams are held accountable by the use of these systems. In my day-to-day interactions with hotel sales executives, I have found that most see the automation as a double-edged sword.

While the industry embraces what technology allows us to do, it is much akin to the tether of the mobile phones and never being able to walk away from work. We enjoy what the technology allows us to do, to quickly and efficiently respond to potential customer needs and questions. However, like any technology, there is an element of abuse. For an insecure or less confident Sales Manager, the technology can be used as a crutch. I always encourage my hospitality clients to remember back to the last time they met face-to-face with a potential customer. The responses are shocking. In more cases than anyone would like to admit, it has been months since they have been on a sales call or set an appointment with a potential client. It is not uncommon for me to meet with a Director of Sales or Sales Manager who has never been on a sales call. The reasons I'm given tend to lean towards the most frequent use of technology. Everything is automated.

There is no need to meet; some clients do not even want to meet. Meeting Planners and Travel Managers are just too busy, and they prefer to rely on the automated systems in place to gather their information and make informed decisions that way.

In that case, let's examine today's Meeting Planner and Travel Manager. What do they look like? What is the typical customer profile? It is hard to tell. Just like most jobs today, consolidation of job duties is a common theme in travel. Companies have scaled back on the number of employees to reduce costs.

Employees are taking on more duties and working many more hours now than they were in the 1990s and even the first part of the 21st century. Meeting planning has been absorbed by various positions including human resources, administrative assistants, procurement/purchasing, or just about anyone that is organized and can take on yet another task.

Few companies have kept their meeting planning departments in-house. Others outsource the meeting planning and travel to third parties who handle hundreds of accounts. The bottom line is that hotel Sales Managers have a difficult enough time even identifying the right person to speak with let alone capturing their attention from all of the other job duties and priorities with which they are tasked. The only apparent theme and commonality among these Meeting Planners and Travel Managers today is that they are overburdened, busy, overworked and many are approaching job burnout.

Of course, they would want to utilize the tools that will help them automate their processes and cut out any unnecessary workload. Automating their processes by using the tools out there to solicit information without direct contact with anyone is perceived to make their job easier. Similarly, many Planners and Travel Managers identify one point of contact from either a hotel brand or a third party Meeting Planner. This helps them to cut back on the phone calls and interaction with sometimes hundreds or thousands of individual hotel Sales Managers.

Imagine being the Meeting Planner for a Fortune 100 company and fielding solicitation calls from every Marriott, every Hilton, and every Holiday Inn in the country?

It is plain to see why hotel sales leadership is frustrated by the sales cycle and process. Hospitality sales professionals are inherently drawn to people. Most likely they were hired for their skill set, which includes as one job posting describes: "excellent communication, presentation, organization, time management and listening skills." They desire face-to-face interaction with potential customers; they want to build relationships and be given the chance to implement their consultative sales skills.

Like in any other industry, they want to sell, but there are giant roadblocks standing in their way. Both the customers and hotel companies have driven the automation of the systems to speed up the communications process and create efficiencies for both groups. Customers simply don't have the time or don't wish to spend their already very limited time listening to sales presentations.

There is a fundamental difference between how hospitality sales professionals want to interact with potential customers and what the buyer's desire is. The key for sales professionals is to bridge the gap between what is required of you as a sales professional to close more business, and how the target customer wishes to interact and ultimately purchase your product and service.

The way to bridge that gap is to give the target customer what they desire. Does that mean automate everything, never pick up the phone, never schedule a face-to-face meeting and rely solely on technology to function as the Sales Manager?

Absolutely not. It means to balance the automation and customer desires of how they prefer to interact with the reality that efficiencies are met by meeting face-to-face when necessary. The skill sets needed for a hotel Sales Manager today are much different because of these changing business dynamics. The face-to-face meeting does not go, but it is not the first step in starting a new business relationship in today's business climate. We will discuss solutions to this challenge of gaining face-to-face meetings or even just attention from target customers. While reviewing these solutions, it is important to realize that the skill sets needed to compete in an automated and consolidated customer world have changed.

The Solution Is to Do the Research

Statistics show high numbers of consumers that research products and services online before purchasing.

Anywhere between 83-94 percent of consumers report they research products online before buying according to internetretailer.com. A corporate executive board study done by Harvard Business Review in 2012 of 1,400 B2B purchasers found that customers are making 60 percent of the buying decision before opening up a conversation with one supplier. That speaks to the importance of making sure websites are accurate, clean and easy to navigate.

However, I think it speaks even more to the world of our target customers. They want to weed out the products and services they do not want first and then have meaningful conversations with their top choices. Because of consolidation, they do not have time to have more than a few conversations, and they use automation to their advantage to minimize the need. That is why building your Sales Toolkits, as Ciara has advised in this book, is so important. These tools are used as a filter. You can either pass the filter test or be left behind.

Doing research is not simply taking a target list of accounts and visiting their websites to fill some knowledge gaps. First, research to understand exactly which target customers are truly a good fit for the hotel product and location. Too often I see hotels will have a long list of target customers that have been passed down from generation to generation of Sales Managers. The accounts may be on the list for many years and no Sales Manager has been able to "crack the code" to gain business from those accounts. Perhaps those accounts should be reviewed and researched to determine if they are a fit for the hotel today. An honest review will bring to light those target accounts that deserve a high level of attention and will help to remove accounts that have been forced due to unrealistic expectations or perhaps outdated information.

Building A Target List of Accounts

Building a list of target accounts through research can be as simple as conducting tele-prospecting, a backyard sales blitz to uncover some of those organizations that are new, have grown or just have simply fallen under the radar. My team at Plan B Consultants conducts The Right Fit Lead™ Prospecting Program for our clients designed specifically to uncover quality clients that fit their target market. Similarly, we handle sales blitz appointment-setting and logistics preparation for hundreds of hotels a year across the U.S., specifically to get out in front of the clients and uncover which ones truly are the right fit for their hotel.

Once a true and realistic set of target customers is identified, a sales team can move on to digging deeper and uncovering what will make the hotel stand out to that customer. In other words, get rid of the noise and focus on what is truly important.

There is unlimited information out there to research target customers. The trickiest part about hiring a Sales Manager and telling them they need to research their target customers and understand their world is that without the proper skill set to do the research effectively, they could end up taking all their time researching and none of their time actually communicating with the client.

I like to use something called "The Red Sheet" to understand what I do not know and still need to uncover for understanding their space. This example is for a hotel just uncovering the basics of a customer they are targeting for individual business travel. I have detailed a link to download this from at the end of this chapter.

Research is not a once-a-year process when building a sales and marketing plan. One piece that my team assists within the research step for our hotel partners is conducting prospecting calls and sales blitzes. This not only identifies the target accounts, but helps Sales Managers to understand key decision factors, competitors, budgets and decision timelines. Outsourcing that initial research allows Sales Managers to focus time effectively.

Other helpful tools for the research step are industry articles about target customers, interviews with current or past employees (these can be very informal), competitive shop calls to discover who they are currently using and at what rates, reading industry reports such as "hotelligence," subscribing to reader boards and joining network groups where the target customers are members. The process of research gets the hotel Sales Manager to a point where they understand the customer enough to speak their language. Information and data gained through this process will be valuable in preparing a business case for each target customer. Business cases use facts and data that provide compelling information as to why a customer should work with a property.

Be Timely

None of the research a hotel conducts will be of value if it is not done in a timely manner. Because 60 percent of the buying process is complete before customers even want to have a conversation, it is vital to get in front of the buying cycle. Part of your research process will be to understand that buying cycle. My team conducts vital research through our prospecting calls to our hotel partners "target suspects" because we ask the following key questions about their decision timeline:

1. When is your next meeting or hotel need?

2. When will you be making the decision for which venue you will use?

3. When and how would you like to be contacted next?

4. Do things change from time to time in your business? Can I contact you again, in say four months' time?

Changing supplier can take up to an average of five contacts, maybe ten. To make it happen, you have to make it as pain-free as possible for the client. You need to think in advance of what obstacles they may come up against to do this – internally and externally. How can you help them educate their meeting planning team about your property for example?

Sometimes timeliness happens by luck. My team makes appointments for hotels to meet up with their target customers all over the U.S. Although a sales blitz is really part of the research step in today's sales cycle, we do luck out and happen to catch customers at the right time in their decision process and win contracts quickly. The key to timeliness is always to be active with the research process. Prospect, network and be out in the community consistently gathering information and sharing the property's information.

Partner with Global or National Sales

Earlier I mentioned that customers often want just one point of contact. Their job has been consolidated, and they do not have time to field calls from hundreds of individual properties. This is why it is important as property Sales Managers to partner with your global or national sales representatives, internally if you have them. Don't go it alone when you do not have to. Educate your partner on the research you have uncovered and they will help you fill in the blanks for that customer and create an even more compelling story to tell. View national or global sales representatives as an internal client. They cannot possibly know every hotel in their portfolio intimately, so educate them on the hotel's attributes and best-fit customers and feed them with valuable and compelling information they can share with target customers.

Similarly, become a partner to the third party Planners and travel management companies that the target clients are working with. Treat them as a partner, speak their language, **know their goals**, and **help them to meet those goals**. Think of it like courting someone you want to date. Sometimes you have to impress the over-protective big brother before you can get the **YES** to the date.

Share Fact-Based Data

The common theme here is that decision-makers are incredibly busy. The days of long lunches to discuss where they want to host their next meeting are gone. As much as some customers may want to be entertained and courted by several hotels for their business, they just don't have the time. Business dynamics have changed, and Meeting Planners and Travel Managers need hotel partners that can speak their language, and collaborate.

Sharing factual information as to why a property is the best choice is important and will capture attention and respect from these busy buyers more than dropping off cookies to their office and sending countless emails requesting a lunch appointment.

Get Yourself an Invite

The best face-to-face appointment with a target customer is when it was their idea to meet. That is when a sales professional knows they have done their job. In today's business climate, the face-to-face where you are truly sitting down and collaborating on how to best conduct business as partners happens as a result of all of the hard work done prior. It includes:

1. Research: prospecting, backyard and feeder market sales blitzes, networking and competitive research of reader boards.

2. Timeliness: sometimes it is the luck of the draw and other times planned timing based on knowledge from the customer research conducted.

3. Global and third party partnerships that can get you a more deeply rooted knowledge-base of the customer and credibility with them.

4. Sharing fact-based data that will certainly gain credibility more quickly by speaking the customer's language and showing that you understand their space.

Action Items from This Section:

- To download a copy of Amy's Red Sheet "Profitable Prospecting Intelligence," go to this address:

www.ConferenceConverter.com/bookresources

- Conduct a sales blitz in your local backyard market. Identify new businesses and start the relationship.
- Update or start your top twenty target list or wish list of clients.
- Download the Perfect Fit Planner™ checklist.

Do you need help with prospecting?
Connect with Amy Infante and her team at this address:
www.planbconsultants.com

What are my top learnings so far?

WONDERFUL
OPPORTUNITY
TO WIN

WOW

How The Sales Role Is Evolving

"I learned More Advanced Sales Techniques that
Work!

I am absolutely delighted with the program. I started
working in hotel sales 12 years ago and just one hour
of your course has shone a big light on how to sell
better and more enjoyably."

Laura Pulling , Abbey Theatre & Events Venue, Dublin, Ireland.

Sales Person Vs Valued Partner

Creating trusted advisors and experts in "How People Gather" instead of sales people.

What is emerging is that sales professionals now need to become educators and consultants. There is a real opportunity for the hotel or venue to become experts in helping a Planner to design their event, to deliver the desired outcomes. A simple question from Jeff Hurt, such as "What will people be doing while in the space?" will help the team to know how to help the Planner.

I have had wonderful discussions with people whom I consider to be thought leaders in this area. People such as Maarten Vanneste, Joan Eisenstodt, Jeff Hurt, Hans Etman and Helen Kuyper. I will share their brilliant points in this chapter.

I have had the pleasure of speaking with a number of hoteliers who really do understand the meetings market. Andy Dolce of Dolce Hotels (now merged with Wyndham Hotels) is client centric. Andy speaks about the level of confidence that the team must build with the Planner in this market. Dolce Hotels' full attention and focus is on doing just that – building confidence with the Planner. His COO, Richard Maxfield referred to it as a "Conference Centric Culture." Richard spoke of the need to understand what the objective of the meeting is and start there instead of focusing on dates, space and rates. I loved Richard's comparison of the hotel industry with the retail market. We have a lot of lessons we can learn from retail.

"Watch how easy they make it to spend more money." Richard remarked. When I thought about it, I thought of an experience I've had at IKEA. You might walk in there to buy a wardrobe, but come out with a whole bedroom suite AND you are delighted you spent the extra money. In my online program on "**How to Write Proposals That WIN**," I share brilliant ideas on how to package the Planner's experience at your venue, so up-sells are seamless. Planners are not afraid to spend money, but they are afraid to waste it.

Most venues sell space according to how many people fit in a room yet they don't understand the real purpose of the meeting, according to Jeff Hurt of Velvet Chainsaw. "We need to flip this question and understand what the real purpose of the meeting or conference is." Then the venue can show the Planner how they can help them achieve that with the variety of furniture options, set-ups and special effects.

Nourishment is a key element also. Dolce Hotels have created Nourishment Hubs, their branded break stations where food is available throughout the day, created in small batches and refreshed regularly. "Thoughtful foods for thoughtful minds" is a wonderful experience created by Andy, Richard and their team at Dolce. Richard spoke of their whole approach as being thoughtful – asking at the beginning of the relationship with the Planner: "What is it you are trying to accomplish?"

Meeting Design is emerging as a key component to any event as Planners struggle to ensure ROI on their event and secure the budget for next year.

A great question from Jeff to ask in opening up a strategic conversation with a Planner is this:

How will you judge the success of this meeting?
Some will judge it by the operational effectiveness of it – how it ran on the day and so on. However, the C-Level Executives and decision-makers will judge success on the strategic success of it, the improved results for their organization. So as hoteliers, we have to start having the conversation around ROI.

According to Jeff: "If hoteliers understand that if a Planner needs to create an environment for authentic conversation, relationship building or transformational experiences, then they can help them to design their event and space to achieve that."

"You must look at space as a blank canvas." It is up to the Planner to design it as an experience, and there is a role for the hotel team to act as a partner in designing this space.

If a Planner answers, "I do not know" when asked one of these two questions:
- What will conference participants be doing in the space?

- What do you want the participants doing or thinking differently after the event?

Then there is an opportunity for the Planner to go back to the decision-makers and ask those questions. What it means for the venue is that the conversation has been turned and is now all focused on strategy rather than rate, space, and dates. By asking the right questions alone, the venue has stood out in the mind of the decision-makers and has got their interest.

If the Planner answers that the attendees will sit and get a lecture in the space, then Jeff points out that there is an opening to turn the conversation to the fact that this conference model does not work anymore for changing people's attitudes or behaviors. It is an information delivery method. It does not mean the audience is learning or agreeing with it.

The Affect and Effect on the Attendee

"The demands of our 21st Century conference participants mandate that we change our traditional event experience. Today's workforce requires that our participants interact, think and work in collaborative ways. Yet our conferences persistently promote expert-directed, one-way passive monologues and panel dialogues."

Jeff Hurt

Check Out Jeff Hurt's Blog on Velvet Chainsaw for more insights in this area.

Joan Eisenstodt, of Eisenstodt Associates, is a fabulous lady in the industry whose expertise is in revitalizing the conference program. She feels there is a big opportunity for hotels and venues to help change the industry.

The hotel is in a position to be an education specialist – understanding meeting design and education. Instead of creating sales people, the venue should be creating a team of people that are consultants to their clients. Advisors in ways that they could deliver a meeting that had a different look, and feel. A meeting that helped accomplish more than what the group thought they could. Joan feels very strongly that venues are missing the opportunity for this change to happen by not helping to educate the Planner.

Richard Maxfield refers to the need for hotels to create a connection and personalize the experience for both the Planner and the participant. Of course there has to be a balance between delivering the WOW and it being practical and profitable.

Space can be used differently; it just takes shaking the cobwebs out of our heads and saying we do not have to sell each room the same. It is not necessarily about having larger space; it is about using the space differently. Joan feels creating the experiential effect involves creating more intimate spaces, changing the way the space is used. The venue provides the couches, the artwork and the effects that soften the look of a cold conference room. The venue should be the expert in their space on what can create a sense of warmth, relaxation or familiarity for the attendee. This helps the group to learn in a way that makes sense to them.

A wonderful expression Joan uses is looking at "how people gather." Follow Joan on her blog or via LinkedIn for more powerful ideas. www.eisenstodt.com

"The impact of the space is so big on people's behaviors it is easier to change the space than the behavior." I just loved the way Helen Kuyper of 24/7 Storytelling, felt so passionately in our conversation about how a venue can impact the outcome of an event. The space instantly changes people's behavior. A certain percentage of the way you behave is defined by your personality, the rest is defined by your surroundings.

A *study presented in Stanford Business Magazine by Christian Wheeler, Associate Professor of Marketing, shows that design cues can put people in a competitive or collaborative frame of mind. A number of studies were carried out in which they exposed individuals to objects common to the domain of business, such as boardroom tables and briefcases, while another group saw neutral objects such as kites and toothbrushes. They then gave all of the participant's tasks designed to measure the degree to which they were in a cooperative or competitive frame of mind.

In every case, participants who were *primed* by seeing the business objects, subsequently demonstrated that they were thinking or acting more competitively. They found that people are more cooperative when they glimpse words like *dependable* and *support* that can be strategically placed in the venue.

"Yes, it was very informative and gave you a different perspective and a new way to think about the Planner and their needs."

Emer Sweeney, Regional Sales Manager City West Hotel & Convention Centre, Dublin, Ireland.

Here are a few pointers from Helen Kuyper of 24/7 Storytelling on how to shake up the traditional use of space and help the Planner deliver results from their conference:

1. Move people around throughout the day. Why? The brain takes a mental image of where we are sitting based on what we are doing. When you change the picture, the brain will refresh, take a new picture and retain more information as the information is associated with a new picture of its surroundings.

However, you cannot just move people around if the space does not allow you to do that. The design of the space influences the ability to do this. The less people carry into a room, the more room there is for people to move. The venue must provide a safe place for people to leave their belongings or they must at least be able to see their bag in order for them to be comfortable moving around freely.

5. If a goal of the conference is for people to collaborate, then setting up the conference room theatre style, isn't going to help them achieve that. Theatre style is only for the transfer of information; it even encourages people to take out their phone and switch off.

6. If at the start of the day, the room is set up theatre style, and the Planner wants people to be collaborative throughout the day, it is too big an ask for people. The room set up at the beginning of the conference must immediately communicate "collaboration" and that this event is going to be different. This prevents attendees "switching off" at the very beginning of the event. The different set up immediately communicates the tone for the day, without even saying a word.

7. Space can anchor what the Planner wants to achieve. Place the stage in the middle of the room. Have different angles from which different presenters present (such as the corners of the room). This creates an air of unexpectedness and again allows the brain to take different pictures, retain and recall more information.

8. Most people are shy at speaking out in large numbers. Help people to share and open up quicker by placing them in smaller groups of five. Get them comfortable participating

in smaller numbers, then have one person give feedback to the room from that table. Once they have shared in a smaller group, it is easier for them to participate within a larger audience.

9. Tables can create barriers. If the Planner needs to create an open space for people to connect, share or come to an agreement at some point throughout the day, then removing the table and seating people in circles will help to achieve this outcome. (I call it a circle of trust in my workshops.)

10. A very simple way to keep people's energy up throughout the day is to show their progress. If the room is changing with you as you go along, then people can see what they have done. The simple act of having attendees work on flip chart paper that can be posted on the wall as they proceed, allows them to reflect, see their progress. This puts the collective brain on display, reminds the group of their progress and this has the effect of keeping their energy and motivation levels up.

11. Using Graphic Illustrators is a fantastic way to reinforce learning and help connect people. They capture in pictures what the presenters are talking about. Place them on the walls, in the hallways or even on the floor where people can walk around them. It helps to create a safe place where people who do not know each other can stand and look at them and comment, opening up conversations with complete strangers. This also has the advantage of helping the brain to remember, recall and apply the learning to their situation. WeThinkVisual.ie based in Cork, Ireland, are a fantastic partner to help bring an event to life visually.

All of the experts I interviewed commented that most venues are transactional versus solution orientated. They are order takers versus order makers. I know from speaking with thousands of hotel and venue sales people worldwide, there is a hunger to change this. By reading this book, you have proven to be one of those, a game-changer in the making in our industry.

Eduardo Chaillo is Global GM Maritz Travel and Honoree at the 2013 Convention Industry Council Hall of Leaders, one conversation with him and you will see why. Eduardo addressed the need for the property contact to be the expert not just in their property but in their area. Linking what is local with the Conference Organizers and participants.

People want to feel connected with the local community. It is a vital emotional experience to bring to events. Connecting meeting attendees not just with the local business people but with the people of the community, in an authentic way. Because it is those stories that he sees conference attendees carry with them, spreading the word when they get back home. Inspiring not just Planners to want to book again, but also their friends, colleagues and neighbors to visit that country.

I had a very interesting conversation with Glenn Miller of IHG. He has managed teams of sales people for twenty plus years. We spoke about the change in the market place in the last twenty years. Mainly with the emergence of 3rd party Agents. (Of which I am one as a Venue Finder!). I haven't spoken specifically about Agents too much in this book. Mainly because they deserve a book dedicated to them!

Glenn makes the following observations. Agents are effectively an intermediary, taking on the role as procurement. They need to see cost containment or cost reduction, so we must present our pricing in that format. The main skill an effective sales person needs to have is to be a problem solver. The Sales person still needs to know why the conference is being held and achieve those goals. However also be a person of business acumen and be creative in helping them to reach their intended goals. Having a friendly relationship is not enough anymore in this market. That skill only "gets you an audience, not a deal."

I have developed a module in my online trainings specifically on how to win more business from Agents. They hold such a position in our industry that they command a module all to themselves. I look forward to sharing the very practical tips from Agents all over the world. I had a particularly engaging conversation with Jason Noah of Great Expectations, London. He shared lots of tips with me on what makes Agents "tick." I got to the heart of the challenges Agents have with hotels and venues with Jacqui Kavanagh of Trinity Conferences. They are such a key link to the conference and event business in this industry. You simply must have a strategy for this valuable source of business. Connect with me if you are interested in learning more about this strategy to WIN.

www.ConferenceConverter.com/agents

When I asked Will Helsby, Director of Sales Great Britain, Best Western Hotels International, what must hotels provide for Conference Organizers in the next three years, he immediately said: "There is too much administration and paperwork imposed on clients. Contracts kill relationships." I have often witnessed that myself as a Venue Finder. Points tend to crop up once the contract appears that were never discussed before. That is why I feel it is very important for the team to introduce the contract earlier in the sales process. Simply saying something like; "Let's talk about commitments now so there are no surprises or delays once we get to that stage." It is a great technique to start to close the sale with, and the Planner appreciates the information up front.

I feel the property could indeed simplify the terms and conditions. As Will points out; "For smaller meetings, the value is the same as 5-6 guest rooms being booked for 2-3 nights. That purchase can be done on the internet, with no contract or strict terms and conditions. We must not introduce these big barriers for the smaller, transactional events."

When speaking with Danny Dolce of LaKota Hotels & Resorts, we spoke of many sales related topics. They are for another book. However, I feel a very important point to share in this chapter is his brilliant point about the organization of the sales team. "We must ensure there are different skill sets on the team. It used to be enough to fill the team with charismatic and rapport building personalities. However, we must address how the big companies source their business now. Requests come from the procurement department first. There are lots of rules and regulations that must be followed to break into these companies. This requires analytical skills, attention to detail and an ability to fill out a very detailed and long form correctly. Not every sales person has these analytical abilities to comply with this paperwork.

Business is lost at these early stages as the procurement department looks at errors in "form filling" as the team not being competent enough to handle their business. Once this step is mastered, business flows."

This conversation with Danny brought me back to my hotel sales days during RFP season, when I had to fill out 200 or so RFPs from September to December during my time in central sales at IHG. Paperwork certainly wasn't my forte.

Practical ideas on how to help Planners design even better events and solve a few problems:

1. **Engage the senses.** How can we engage the attendees' senses by just walking into a room?

   Feel: Does the floor covering feel different? Is it softer? Or plusher?

   Smell: Are our senses awakened by a different scent? The sharp scent of citric or a calming scent of lavender?

   Vision: Perhaps a rotating banner or changing display on the wall?

   Music/Audio: Music has an immediate impact of movement and bringing up people's energy levels. Jeff Hurt even has his own theme music at events. I do love that touch.

2. Joan Eisenstodt recommends the book *Seating Matters* by Paul O. Radde. It explores how to **change standard seating** and keep it people centric. Joan emphasizes that if venues are coming up with ideas for the client, then the client will want to work with the venue. It helps eliminate the competition.

3. If you know the **goal of the meeting**, then you know the style of the lunch. I loved this suggestion by Hans Etman of Masters in Moderation. He suggests a picnic style lunch if the goal of the meeting is to get people to connect and network. Have picnic baskets set up for tables of four or so attendees who can help each other to lunch and even make their own sandwiches.

   If the goal is to have employees feel they are appreciated, set the room up restaurant style and have the board of directors serve their teams. It can be gourmet food or simple food. It does not matter as long as it is good and honest food.

4. If the event is **bringing people together**, who have met before, then a goal is to help them reconnect and share. Hans suggests making the food family style, with more casual tablecloths set in such a way that people can feel comfortable to move around. If it is an international company bringing together different offices, perhaps have the different countries suggest a recipe and serve those throughout the event. If venues are helping the client create a very personalized menu for their event, with serving suggestions on how to create the right atmosphere, then they have the client's attention.

Joan Eisenstodt, who is not just a trainer in this area but who also runs conferences for clients, suggests that she would love to see venues package themselves with this mindset and approach to delivering conferences instead of packaging with pricing.

The conversation in the meetings market is moving to how the venue can help the Planner design the experience, so people remember it, retain it and apply it. The future of events is all about how people apply their learning back on the job.

"If the transfer between what attendees hear/learn/ experience at a meeting or conference and how they apply it to their job does not happen, then the meeting has failed and the venue is death by relationship."

Jeff Hurt

The industry is changing, the way events are delivered is changing, but it is not happening instantly. It is going to take a few years for this to become commonplace. Your opportunity is here. Now. Get ahead of the curve and adapt this approach to selling space.

"I've reviewed the approach Ciara trains hotels and venues to use to reach and work with Conference Planners effectively. It's brilliant. If hotels and venues made it that easy for me to book my conferences with them, it would save me days of time and a lot of stress. I'd love them for it."

Katja Keil, Conference Planner, NoSQL Matters, Germany

Having these strategic level conversations with the Planner will not just happen instantly. Mastering the first three steps as I outlined in the opening chapters of this book, building the right level of trust and confidence with the Planner, must be done correctly first. This creates the right environment for the Planner to be open to these high level, strategic, meaningful conversations. You cannot just jump into them. You have to take it step, by step as outlined in my "**7 Step Conference Converter System™**." Conversations at this level, start happening around step 3-4 of my system, once this strong foundation of trust is in place.

This approach to the sales efforts in the conference and meetings market will help venues to catapult themselves into the role of being a partner instead of being a supplier. Being a partner is a lot more lucrative.

Thank you for your time in reading this book. I am honored.
If you would like to learn more about how to develop these sales skills and become a rock star in your industry, connect with me. I would welcome a conversation with you.
win@ConferenceConverter.com

What are my top learnings so far?

WONDERFUL
OPPORTUNITY
TO WIN

WOW

"The 7 Steps to WIN provides hotels the perfect insight and understanding into *'what client's want and need'* during the sales process.
Ciara's training platform will allow the hotels to:

- engage in a much more proactive way with clients
- have a much stronger understanding of the client's needs and expectations
- convert more business and
- make the client journey that much better."

Justine Thomas-Butler, Head of Meetings, Incentives & Events, Arabian Adventures, a DMC, PCO Company, Dubai.

"Finally a 'how to' book on how to build and train a sales team to **increase sales and market share**.

Ciara has really "nailed it" with the details on how to build trust with your clients and prospects, **develop effective sales tools and use technology** as an effective tool to **WIN** new business.

Her introduction of the **Client Converter Toolkit™** and cycle was particularly interesting to me as an owner and operator of group centric hotels and resorts. This is an approach that can be adapted by our sales people that will build trust with their clients and keep them coming back.

I know that you will enjoy reading this book and use it as a **tool in the training of your sales organization**."

Andy Dolce, Owner Operator, Dolce Hotels and Resorts, voted one of the 25 Most Influential Executives in the Meetings Industry

If you would like to help your team to master the sales skills outlined in this book, connect with me. I would welcome a conversation with you.

Ciara

win@ConferenceConverter.com

Bibliography

Books:

Achor, Shawn. *Happiness Advantage*. Random House, Inc., 2010.
Kline, Nancy. *More Time to Think*. Fisher King Publishing, 2009.
Radde, Paul O. *Seating Matters*. Thriving Publications, 2009
Vanneste, Maarten. *Meeting Architecture: A Manifesto*. Meeting Design Institute, 2008.

Reports/Articles:

Abstract. "Air Quality." The U.S. Natural Library of Medicine.
Hill, Ruth. "Getting up to Speed on Event Bandwidth." Convention Industry Council (CIC) and Hospitality Sales and Marketing Association International (HSMAI) (2013).
"Inspirational Hotel of the Future." Best Western Members Conference (2015)
Latham, James. "The Wisdom of Crowds." International Meetings Review.
Harvard Review Study. "A recent Corporate Executive Board study of more than 1,400 B2B customers found that those customers completed, on average, nearly 60% of a typical purchasing decision before even having a conversation with a supplier." Harvard Business Review Study.
Wheeler, Christian & Associates. "Design Cues." Stanford Business Magazine.

Websites:

"Prescriptive Energy Code Checklist,"
www.energy.wsu.edu

"Business cards for each staff member,"
www.smartguests.com/blog/all-hospitality-people-need-business-cards-business-cardstop-5-reasons-why/#.V9guS_ArLIU

"CO2 levels,"
www.engineeringtoolbox.com/co2-persons-d_691.html

"Convention Industry Council APEX Standards Committee Bandwidth Estimator,"
www.speedtest.net

"Convention Industry Council APEX Standards Committee Bandwidth Estimator,"
www.speakeasy.net/speedtest

"Digital Marketing Blog,"
www.blog.hubspot.com/marketing/visual-content-marketing-strategy#sm.00008yr0ny2zzd6yqwh1hzgxvhrby

"Disney on Projection Mapping,"
www.youtube.com/watch?v=3ycK8LWEN-c

"Natural Light and the Brain,"
www.examinedexistence.com/lighting-and-its-affect-on-your-mood

"Research on a One Minute Video,"
www.forrester.com/report/How+Video+Will+Take+Over+The+World/-/E-RES44199

"Room Capacity numbers,"
www.MPIweb.org

"Video Marketing Statistics,"
www.syndacast.com

"What do venues do that drives you mad?"
www.linkedin.com

Acknowledgements

In this book I share many ideas on how to build a rock solid foundation to your whole sales approach. I start with showing you the roots through to creating a winning sales strategy. That is - understanding how your client is thinking. This is the foundation of solid sales skills. It's the beginning of mastering the meetings market.

This analogy of rock solid foundations made me think about my roots and my own foundations. They come from my parents – Ursula and Barry Feely. I was lucky enough to have grown up in a loving household; that was a very traditional Irish home. My Dad was the bread winner and we were very fortunate to have Mam stay home and dedicate herself to her family. My mother was always there for her five children and for Dad. She was consistent and resourceful and still is. I know now that I picked up a lot of those skills from her. They are skills that are essential to running your own business. Consistency is also what gets you results in the meetings market.

My Dad ran his own business; he has the entrepreneurial flair. I always visualized being a business woman, doing my own thing. Dad has a passion for what he does – working in the stone industry. He 'found himself' once he started working with his hands. Carving stone in his apprentice days and moving on to building an international stone company. Dad has been even more of an inspiration in the last ten years having written four books in his semi-retirement years – despite the fact that he is dyslexic.

I've definitely brought that lesson of being passionate about what you do to my business. I have found what I love doing, what makes me jump out of bed in the morning. I teach the importance of being passionate about your property and your business and tapping into that passion when working with clients, particularly in the meetings market.

I thank my parents for giving me my wings from an early age.

(Picture of my Dad and I with a few neighbors in Greatmeadow, Boyle, Co. Roscommon, Ireland)

To my sister Rhona, who got all the spelling genes in the family! Thank you for always helping out and answering the many texts I sent you to check the spelling of a word, or the structure of a sentence.

To my cousin Edel Hopkin, who proofread a few sections of the Sales Toolkit when I first started to write. Thank you! I didn't realize how bad my grammar was until I saw your edits!

I must mention our twin boys Jack and Aaron. Who are now six but were three when I started to write this book. The Sales Toolkit chapters were written as I waited outside their pre-school on a Monday, parked in a field overlooking beautiful country views for two and a half hours. I needed to maximize my writing time so I chose to sit there rather than to go back to the office and waste time driving. I thank them for sleeping in until eight most mornings so I could get two hours of writing done before we started our day together. Although on the mornings they got up early the extra snuggles on the couch were precious. Jack and Aaron you are my driving force.

My rock is my lovely husband Michael. He has never wavered; never lost faith in me, even on the days that I was close to giving up. He never asked me to stop doing what I was doing. Especially when my business wasn't making any money. He always believes in me and that support means so much to me. It has kept me going. **I love and thank you Michael.**

Contributors to This Book

Writing this book has given me the opportunity to speak with some of the most amazing people in the industry.

I had the pleasure of speaking with **Andy Dolce** in January of 2014. He is the owner and operator of Dolce Hotels, a group of extremely conference centric hotels and resorts. It was refreshing to meet a hotelier with such a client perspective who holds the distinction of being named one of the "25 Most Influential Executives" in the meetings and travel industries by both *Meeting News* and *Business Travel News* magazines. Andy spoke of the importance of hoteliers developing the mindset of building a level of confidence with the Meeting Planner so their full attention can be on their participants. That is true partnership with the Planner in delivering all of their meeting objectives. He very kindly connected me with other fascinating members of his team that I have had very interesting conversations with.

Thank you to **Richard Maxfield, Dolce Hotels COO, Ted Brumleve, Director Technical Services of Dolce Hotels, John Evans, GM at the Silverado Dolce Hotel and Danny Dolce Senior**

VP, LaKota Hotels and Resorts for your time and expertise in helping me develop the chapters on space design and creating a conference centric culture. I thoroughly enjoyed our conversations and very much appreciate your generous sharing of your genius. I can see why Dolce Hotels and Resorts are setting the pace in this market.

Andy also connected me with **Richard Penner, Cornell Hotel School of Design** and **Simon Turner, President, Global Development of Starwood Hotels & Resorts Worldwide, Inc.;** both of whom I interviewed for their expertise in hotel design and what works on a practical and profitable level. Your time is very much appreciated.

Thank you **Virginia Cantillon** who introduced me to **Seamus O'Mahony** who introduced me to Andy Dolce. Great things can come out of getting up at 5 am every Friday morning to attend a BNI networking event.

When I started to write this book, I knew what I needed to get out of my head. It was everything I had experienced as being the client that I knew could be done more effectively by hotels and venues. But I needed help. I needed help to get it to another level. I started to educate myself on what was the next wave in the industry. I started reading a lot of blogs, following people on social media and attending events. I love that about our industry, you just have to get out there and meet people.

One of my early influencers in the industry was **Maarten Vanneste of The Meetings Institute**. I later discovered Maarten wrote a book in 2007 on the topic of designing meetings and their content. In it he focuses on "what happens during the meeting that is important to meeting owners - the meeting initiators, and their objectives. What changes in the minds of the participants, what influences the participants, what supports the objectives of the meeting in terms of learning, networking and motivation." I loved our conversations and I thank you Maarten for sharing your time and expertise.

Andy Bounds (voted number 1 sales trainer in the UK) has had a big impact on my business and on my thinking. I call him the "AFTER's Man." His ethos is this: "How much better off are your clients after you have worked with them?" His insights have helped me to develop my perspective and teach hotels how to win more. I knew what I needed to say from being the client, but Andy's teachings helped me to make it easy to teach that to my clients. For that reason, I asked him to contribute a chapter to my book. When this technique is applied to your business, it works.

I spoke with **Deborah Gardner**, a performance expert. She made a strong analogy that the early stages of engaging with a client is a little like dating. You have to make an impression, you have to WOW them and pull them in. You have to make them want a second date. Andy shows us how to do this in the all-important proposal. Thank you Deborah for your insights. I look forward to attending one of your inspiring events.
www.DeborahGardner.com

Amy Infante is a friend and colleague since 2001. We worked together at the Omni San Francisco Hotel. She is a digger. She was brilliant at uncovering new business, researching and prospecting. She has since built a very successful business doing just that for hotels internationally. She has a team of people who research and uncover business opportunities for hotels all day, every day. She was the perfect person to contribute to this book.

Prospecting is not dead. Finding more of the right kind of clients (**Right Fit Leads™**) is seriously profitable. She shares her valuable insights in the chapter on "**The Perfect Fit Planner™.**" A big thanks to you Amy for all your support and "chats" so far. I know we will continue to do great work together in the industry.

I was so excited when I met **Fiona McDonald** of Spatial Design one morning at a BNI event. I shared with her what I was thinking about a venue, the room in particular and how that can have a big outcome on an event. She is a 'Space Architect' and an observer of how people use space. She said something to me that really stuck with me: "**space communicates a message.**" That is the title and the foundation of my chapter on what I find a most fascinating topic.

I even learned from Fiona that the conference room can influence how people learn, retain and apply information. I think you will love that chapter. I interviewed several experts for this chapter and distilled the best ideas to make them relevant and easy to apply to client conversations. Thank you Fiona for kick-starting it for me.

A big thanks to Architects **James Dilley of Jestico + Whiles** and **Amy Jakubowski of Wilson Associates, Los Angeles** for sharing your brilliant hotel design ideas.

Niki Schafer, an Interior Designer who shared her ideas about what doesn't work when designing networking space.

Ben Goedegebuure for sharing your practical experience with opening and operating the Scottish Exhibition and Convention Centre and as Global GM of Maritz Europe, Middle East and Africa.

My husband **Michael Cahalane** is a Passive House build specialist and he wrote a section on a very easy way to help meeting participants get over the 3pm slump. It's all to do with the air!

I just loved speaking with Congress Planners who want and see the benefit of all of this knowledge. Thank you to Ciara Mundrow and Chelsea Thomas of the European Society of Cardiology for your time. It was great to have practical conversations about the application of all of this at your events.

Thank you to **Katja Keil** of No SQL Matters, **Justine Thomas-Butler** of Arabian Adventures, **Rick Thompson** of FORUM Institut for Management for sharing your perspective, as the Planner.

A big thanks to **Jacqui Kavanagh** of Trinity Conferences, for sharing how hotels just have to make life easier for their clients. I hope I got them all in the Sales Toolkit Step.

I met **Ann Hansen** at the MPI EMEC Conference 2016. The design of the event was very impactful. It introduced fun and a lot of audience participation. I was thrilled to see so much of what I wrote about in action. At the last minute on my request she contributed thoughts on communicating content through emotions and tactility in meetings. It was the missing piece. Thank you Ann. www.ahcc.dk

I am proud to say that I have brought the best ideas from real thought leaders in our industry together in the last chapter on "How the Role of the Sales Team is Evolving." **Jeff Hurt, Joan Eisenstodt, Maarten Vanneste, Helen Kuyper and Hans Etman.** Thank you.

Jeff Hurt writes a thought provoking blog on Velvet Chainsaw. If you want to know the way conferences are going – follow Jeff!

Joan Eisenstodt is a fabulous lady in the industry who feels there is a big opportunity for hotels and venues to help change the industry. I love her phrase about creating trusted advisors and experts in "how people gather." I can't wait to meet you in person and deliver this book Joan. My sincere thanks to you for your generous sharing. www.Eisenstodt.com

I attended **Helen Kuyper's** workshop on storytelling. I just loved the way she used the blank canvas of space to help us design and build our story. I just knew I had to share her wisdom in this book. Helen shares lots of simple, practical ideas in this chapter on "How people Gather." A big thank you Helen. I look forward to doing another workshop with you. www.24-7Storytelling.com

Hans Etman shares ideas about such detail as if you know the goal of the meeting, then you know the style of lunch to recommend. The Food and Beverage team have a big impact on the outcomes of a meeting. Thank you Hans for taking the time to share your ideas. www.MastersinModeration.com

Glenn Miller, Director of Regional Sales and Marketing, IHG. I just loved your summary of what today's sales person needs to be – "A problem solver." "Being friendly just isn't enough anymore, that gets you an audience, not a deal."

Shawna Suckow, Founder of SPIN, Author and Speaker – a group of senior Planners. When interviewing her for this she told me Planners just don't believe traditional sales and marketing messages any more. I loved our conversation as we have both experienced the same frustrations as being the client. Thanks a million for your time. www.SpinPlanners.com

I asked **Corbin Ball** to contribute to this chapter as he is recognized as one of the Top 25 Most Influential People in the Meetings Industry and has been for years. He is top of his game when it comes to Conference Technology and the recognized "Go to Expert" in this area worldwide. He shares his view of what is hot in the technology of meetings right now.

I met **Brandt Krueger** at ibtm world. I attended one of his talks, which was brilliant. He just made the application of technology easy and practical. That is what he has shared with us in the chapter on creating your Tech Toolkit. He had me captivated when he demonstrated the possibilities of projection mapping and all I could see was the possibilities that had for the Meetings & Event Industry. Thank you Brandt for sharing your brilliance.

James Corbett was introduced to me through Ciara Crossan of Weddingdates.co.uk. I saw immediately the possibilities that Google Cardboard had for the industry. James was the tech person who made it happen every day for his clients. Thank you for explaining it in a non-techy way James, in your contribution on "Technology to help the Planner visualize their event at your Venue."

I met **Jean-Christophe Chemin of 45° Nord Consulting**, a Venue Finding Agency based in France. We met while doing a hotel tour at 8pm on a January evening in Dublin. I remarked: "at least I wasn't the only one that loved looking around hotels in their spare time." We both laughed as we shared that passion for checking out hotels for clients. Thank you for sharing what frustrates you about trying to find a venue and how hotels and venues can ultimately make life easy for the Planner by giving more details upfront on the website and in the proposal.

Thank you to the **Convention Industry Council, HSMAI and APEX** for allowing me to share the white paper prepared by **Ruth Hill**, "Getting up to Speed on Event Bandwidth.

Rose Gowan of RoseGowan.com for a great profile picture and **Andy Rogers of Xpedient Print.co.uk**, thank you for your tips on powerful print. I share all of your wisdoms in detail in my online program on how to build a Marketing Toolkit to attract better quality leads: **www.ConferenceConverter.com/connect**

Vincent Walshe of InternetSuccess.ie. Thank you for our many hours of idea sharing. Your support over the last two years as I transformed my business has been invaluable.

Rupesh Patel of SmarterGuests.com – thanks for your brilliant ideas on how hoteliers can gather more authentic sales material – testimonials!

Jason Noah MD of Great Expectations, a UK based Agency. I look forward to sharing your brilliant tips on how hotels can win more business from Agents in my next book. I've a whole module dedicated to it on: **www.ConferenceConverter.com/agents**

Jessie States, Manager of Education, MPI. For your patient attention to detail and journalist editing talent, I am indebted to you. Thank you for giving up your free time to do that. Thank you for your support and partnership in launching the MPI Venue Sales Certificate Program. I am proud that my system and teachings have passed this level of professional education in our industry. Thank you for spotting the 'diamond in me', as you put it.

I know **Derek Reilly** through BNI (Business Network International). In 2011 he originally suggested that I teach hotels how to do what I do in my Venue Finding business. As a mother of 15-month-old twins at the time, I just couldn't see how I could possibly do one more thing. You planted the seed even though I didn't realize it at the time. And look what that seed bloomed into. Thank you for that conversation.

Rick Armstrong, my publisher. Who patiently waited three years, even though I was sure I'd have it done in 6 months! Thank you for your support, faith and brilliant ideas. Thank you for sending me Nancy Kline's book; it was a source of inspiration to me, in particular the chapter on "Space to Think."

Paul O'Mahony of @omaniblog is always an interesting man to have a conversation with. He really helped me to see that I looked at venues in a different way to the venue team. I look at a hotel from the client's perspective. That turned around my business and led me on this path. Thank you Paul.

I met **Eduardo Chaillo** on Twitter, then in person at ibtm world. Eduardo is Global GM Maritz Travel and Honoree at the 2013 Convention Industry Council Hall of Leaders, one conversation with him and you will see why. I look forward to sharing more of his insights in my online module on how to **WIN** more business from Agents.

Thank you to **Pádraic Gilligan** of Sool Nua, **Micah Solomon** and **Vikram Singh** for your time spent in conversations about how hotels can win more, what to put on their website and advice on writing a book.

I must mention **Jeanine Blackwell** who is a brilliant teacher on how to write a course online. I've shared some of your wisdom in the testimonial section. It's wonderful learning from you.

The people who shared with me and whose contributions will be in my next book. I just couldn't fit in all the brilliant ideas into the one book. Thank you to **Dan O'Donoghue, Scot Cuthbertson, Mary Menton** and **Charlie Sheil**, GM Marker Hotel, Dublin, Ireland. My next book will focus on the Sales System and "Building a Healthy Sales Funnel." Your contributions in this area and in great conference food Charlie are noted.

I feel honored to have shared a conversation with such distinguished professionals as are noted above.

I must also mention the hundreds of Conference, Meeting and Event Planners I learned so much from as a Venue Finder. Understanding your business and the challenges you face has given me a whole new business and perspective.

The Story of How I Got to "Here"

I am a hotelier by heart. Joey Miranda Oliva (now of Highgate Hotels) hired me into this industry in 1996 as Sales Coordinator for the central sales office of Bristol Hotels, which became InterContinental Hotels. We sold five hotels in downtown San Francisco, sixty conference rooms and about 2500 guestrooms. I was lucky to have a number of mentors with that company. Sheila Fonseca and Marie Allen, my first managers, and Joey the head of our division. Thank you ladies, for your guidance, lessons and friendship.

I've had very influential Directors of Sales and Marketing with that company whom I still consider my mentors. Sheila Foley who has gone on to be General Manager of the Arizona Biltmore Hotel, a Waldorf Astoria Hotel and Dayna Zeitlin who is blazing a trail with Provenance Hotels.

Dayna hired me to help her open the Omni San Francisco Hotel in 2001. That was a career highlight for me as we built sales revenue from zero to $5.8 million in my first year and I loved every minute of it. I was particularly proud of that figure especially opening the hotel three months after 9/11. I still consider that hotel my baby as it was such a tough competitive market to sell in. I learned a lot.

Dayna taught me the importance of building trust and focusing on the team. She looked after her team as well as she did her clients. With her as a role model I treated my clients with that same level of respect and appreciation for their business.

I can still hear Sheila Foley coming out of her office at 10am saying: "It's prime selling time ladies, are you talking to your clients?" I quote you regularly Sheila. A common characteristic of great sales people is that they respect prime selling time. It is for client conversations only.

Tracie Lundquist Gunning was my first partner in business. I was promoted to Sales Manager and we were teamed up together. She was the first person to teach me to stop selling and build the relationship first. I also learned a lot from her about the importance of having fun in business. Jim McGuire and Tracie were definitely role models in how to reach your sales goals while having a lot of fun with your clients and members of your team.

I will always remember the wise words of **John Simonich a Regional Vice President of Operations at InterContinental Hotels**: "Ciara, selling a hotel is a lot like selling perishable goods. If you don't sell a guest or meeting room today, the opportunity is lost forever." I've always looked at hotel sales from that perspective, the opportunity lost. It's helped me to focus on the conversion rate.   A key area I help my clients grow.

In our industry, the average conversion rate is 20 percent. That means that 80 percent of the sales effort is not productive. That adds up to a lot of empty guestrooms and meeting rooms.

Wasted sales effort and empty rooms is costing the industry billions in lost revenue opportunities every year. This book was written out of pure frustration in seeing why business is being lost. I only saw the reasons why so much business is lost, once I became the client however.

I've been a Venue Finder for ten years. I developed this niche for myself after moving back to Ireland. I founded FindaConferenceVenue.com in 2006, where I run both an online directory for finding venues and a personal service. In that capacity I listened to the client brief – asked very detailed questions such as what are the results you want to get from organizing this event? I wrote very detailed specifications that I sent out to suitable hotels and venues. What I found was the proposal sent to me was rarely enough to convince the Planner why I felt the recommended hotel was at least worth a site inspection.

I had to do all this work in the middle, rewrite the descriptions, and make **it so easy for the Planner** to see why the venue was the right fit. I prepared hundreds of reports for the client to convince them why I was recommending a property. I sometimes had to hop into the car and go take my own photos and videos of the property.

I saw first-hand why business was being lost and I wanted to do something about it. So I started to write this book. That is when I saw there was a difference between how the property wants to sell and how the Planner wants to buy. I developed the **Conference Converter System™**, to bridge that gap. The system is proven, it makes sense, it's practical and it works.

Planners have told me that if hotels and venues sold the way I recommend; it would make their life so much easier. We all want to work with people who make our life easier right?

Now during my hotel career, even though I was promoted and was responsible for budgets of millions of dollars, I also made lots of mistakes. And I can see them clearly now that I look at the business from the Conference Planners perspective.

I worked in Ireland and the US during my hotel career. While I concentrated on constantly finding new clients, I never paid much attention to the tools I was using to attract these clients in the first place. And the biggest mistake I made is that I was selling. I did all the company sales training programs, but when I became the client I realized that all my training was on how to sell from the hotels point of view, not on how the Planner wanted to buy. I didn't take the time to step back and look at what I was doing and saying from the client's point of view.

Planners Have Changed the Way They Buy, Have You Changed the Way You Sell?

And now that I can see from being a Venue Finder, that it is a completely different point of view. The industry has changed dramatically in the last number of years so the approach you take has to change too. That is what I teach. I can show you how to create the right sales tools that will give you a much more powerful position with the Planner. I can show you how to approach the Conference, Meeting and Event Planner the way they want to be approached. The way that will help you build relationships that will result in more business being won.

Now as a Venue Finder, I have heard thousands of pitches, been on too many websites researching venues and I've been sent hundreds of sales brochures. I have also received thousands of proposals. It's rare that I receive a brilliant one. The one thing most of them have in common is they are all about the venue instead of being all about the client. I turn that around in this book and in my online programs and workshops.

The Next Step

I specialize in showing hotel and venue sales teams how to think like their client. How to build the right tools that decision-makers use every day to help them make a decision. This book is just one part of how I create those transformations in a sales team's approach to this market.

I have found after three years of working with teams that results happen quicker when I work with teams over a longer period of time – sharing small amounts of information, then checking for learning, understanding and application. Most questions come up after the trainer leaves the room. If they are not answered, the team will go back to their old way of doing things. The revenue transformation will not take place. **Most training fails because there is no follow-up or implementation plan.** I make sure to work with the team until they are comfortable and confident in adopting a new way of thinking and selling.

I've adopted a 4-way method of ensuring your return on investment. It's my top selling program as it's the way I drive revenue results quicker (as much as $250,000 within 6 weeks of the program). This is what makes it work:

1. The team gets access to my online programs – a training website with new modules released in a planned timescale.

2. Then we have regular live Q&A sessions in the form of webinars, where we reinforce the learning and start building confidence in adopting this.

3. Then I introduce one on one mentoring sessions so it is tailor-made for each person and they feel they are getting their own questions answered that they may be shy to ask in a group scenario.

4. Then I go there in person, most of the mindset shift has happened at this stage so a day's training is a lot more productive. We are tweaking, working on real-life examples of clients and creating sales tools just for your team.

And now there is the book!

It's not enough to just tell someone something. Once teams have developed a habit in the way they sell, it takes time to break those habits and most importantly build confidence in adopting a new approach.   That is why I love to work with clients in the above order. Of course, there is an *á la carte* option too.

I am committed to getting results, that is my ethos, that is my drive for your team.

www.ConferenceConverter.com/connect

Ciara Feely, Creator of The Conference Converter System™

The Industry Expert in showing hotels and venues how to **WIN** More Profitable Business and Market Share with the 7 Steps to **WIN!**
Ciara@ConferenceConverter.com

Lightning Source UK Ltd.
Milton Keynes UK
UKOW06f0043020317
295715UK00013B/58/P

9 781910 406458